THE ROAD TAKEN

Men, Motorcycles and Me

THE ROAD TAKEN

Men, Motorcycles and Me

A Memoir

Linda Dodwell

GALAH PRESS

ISBN: 978-1-953596-22-2 (paperback)
ISBN: 978-1-953596-23-9 (e-book)

Library of Congress Cataloging-in-publication data
The Road Taken: Men, Motorcycles and Me, Dodwell, Linda

Photo credit, pp. 209-210, Blake Thompson
Cover Design by Eric Labacz

Galah Press
Glen Ellen, California

Printed in the United States of America

For my daughter Maida.
By far the best road taken.

I shall be telling this with a sigh
Somewhere ages and ages hence:
Two roads diverged in a wood, and I—
I took the one less traveled by,
And that has made all the difference.

—Robert Frost, "The Road Not Taken"

Foreword

Twenty-six years ago, I met Linda Dodwell in Melbourne, Australia as she was co-leading a motorcycle tour "Down Under" with Geoff Coat. I had retired from my architectural practice and had begun Lotus Tours, an international motorcycle touring company. My Australian motorcycle tour was really a research trip to see how other folks ran their tours. Our company slogan was: "You supply the helmet – we supply the adventure." And boy was Linda ready for adventure!

Linda and I have shared plentiful motorcycle adventures in France, India, Italy, Mexico, South Africa, and Spain. Linda was also a participant in the 16,000-kilometer Peking to Paris Rally that I had entered, which was a heroic undertaking lasting almost two months on the road.

While I thought I knew a lot about Linda from the many social encounters with groups of fellow travel enthusiasts over the years, reading her memoir certainly opened many windows into her past. *The Road Taken: Men, Motorcycles, and Me* is a pleasure to read and entices the reader to rush forward to the next chapter. Linda's self-confidence, sense of adventure, and can-do attitude are dominant in her evolution as someone who does not take "no!" for an answer. Her memoir introduces you to the many aspects of her life that is clearly a life full of accomplishments.

As an architect myself, I had no idea of her three-dimensional visions about house improvements and ambitious renovations Linda has undertaken. Linda is no shrinking violet! She is an amazingly competent, capable person who has a unique background as a problem-solver with a great sense of humor.

From nursing to earning an art degree and learning to pilot a motorcycle at the age of forty-four to becoming a world traveler takes a lot of guts, courage, and determination.

Linda's complexity as an accomplished woman jumps off the pages and out of the book, inspiring all of us to do the same.

Burt Richmond
Founder and Tourmeister,
Lotus Tours

Table of Contents

CHAPTER 1

Hackensack
-Laguna Beach-Hackensack

1944-1950

Some lives roll out smoothly like a nicely paved road traveling in a straight line from cradle to grave. Not mine. My life tumbled out like a sack of rocks on a chaotic path that turned and twisted, endlessly marked by exhilarating triumphs and sobering defeats.

On the day I was born, December 8, 1944, World War II was raging and the man who fathered me, Hilbert Walter Dodwell (everyone called him Dod), was in the South Pacific on the Solomon Islands, bravely serving his country as a Staff Sargent in the U.S. Marine Corps. While far away, in a hospital in Hackensack, New Jersey, surrounded by female relatives without the comfort of a husband present, my mother, Margaret Elizabeth Ann McGivney (Margo), labored to bring me into the world.

I was the first grandchild for both my maternal and paternal grandparents and upon arrival I became an instant celebrity. Due to the war, the early months of my life were spent without a father. Dod and Margo had married shortly before he was shipped off to Bougainville; the last of the Solomon Islands to be recaptured from the Japanese. It was a scary time and American wives were encouraged to put on "a brave face" and avoid the terrifying truth that their husbands were in daily combat with an enemy whose sole purpose was to annihilate them. Young mothers, like mine, moved back in with their parents to have some sense of communal comfort and the family unit was redefined around the absence of fathers, many of whom would never return.

On August 1, 1945, America dropped an atomic bomb on Hiroshima, Japan, and five days later a second bomb on the city of Nagasaki, bringing a swift end to the war and unleashing a flood of nightmare scenarios about this terrifying new weapon, which held a real possibility for the complete destruction of mankind. The "father of the bomb," Robert Oppenheimer, acknowledged his accountability by quoting Hindu scripture, *"Now I am become Death, the destroyer of worlds."* More than 200,000 dead Japanese civilians, many of them burned beyond recognition, validated his claim.

This was the apocalyptic world I was born into. Perhaps it's the reason uncertainty has always seemed normal to me. I was primed from birth to know that nothing was permanent and life altering changes often came suddenly – and in frightening ways.

On September 2, 1945, when I was almost nine months old, the Japanese Emperor Hirohito, formally signed a declaration of surrender aboard the United States Navy battleship *USS Missouri* and a sigh of relief swept across America. Our brave troops were shipped home and loved ones rushed to embrace the returning heroes. My father was among them. As Dod used to say, he was discharged from the Marine Corps "when they shut down the war."

Dod's release from duty came in San Diego, California, and my mother left Hackensack, New Jersey, carrying me in her arms and flew out to meet him. It was the first of what would be many far-flung journeys for me and as I've been told, I cried and screamed throughout the entire flight. I can only surmise that it was the pain of teething or the cabin pressure on my tender eardrums, but the discomfort of that trip made for a story that my mother, Margo, repeated – far too often.

I have no conscious recollection of meeting my father. They say the practical function of memory doesn't begin until the age of two or three, but even experts agree that memories suffused with great emotion are likely to form earlier and last longer. The emotional reunion of my parents, Dod and Margo, no doubt had a powerful effect on me. Still in their mid-twenties, they were two innocent young people who had barely started their life together before the war ripped them apart. The early bonding that comes from going through a pregnancy and the birth of a first child together was denied them and I don't know that they ever got their footing as a married couple. When they reunited, they were in many ways strangers to each other; their awkwardness was now compounded by a squalling infant and whatever emotional baggage the war had left them with. It made for a rocky start.

I'm sure my mother would have preferred to immediately return to the safety of her family life in New Jersey, but my father had already found a job as a police officer in Laguna Beach. With so many servicemen being discharged at the same time, jobs were scarce and he felt fortunate to find work that suited him. His Marine training was perfect for police work. The Chief of Police took a liking to this handsome and personable young man and provided us with a basement apartment beneath his own home on Ruby Street in Laguna Beach.

The Dodwells settled into married life taking full advantage of the Southern California lifestyle. A swimmable beach was reached by a public path just the other side of the highway. Dod and Margo were avid body surfers and I was often left on a blanket on the sand while they frolicked in the waves. Years later, Margo would wonder why they felt no compunction about leaving a child alone on the beach. I often wondered the same thing. Was it because they were more interested in having a good time than being responsible parents? Or was it because even at that tender age I had already shown that I could take care of myself. I chose to believe it was the latter.

Laguna Beach was a magical place, with Hollywood a scant sixty miles away; near enough for movie stars to own homes along the lush and dramatic coastline. Betty Grable, the famed Hollywood musical star and WWII pinup girl, along with her equally famous husband, trumpeter and bandleader, Harry James, lived close enough so that their house was viewable from our Ruby Street location. The movie connection became even stronger when Dod was approached by a man claiming to be a Hollywood agent, who suggested he might find him work as a double for Rory Calhoun, a movie heartthrob who starred in westerns and romantic films. Dod was flattered, head shots were taken, but nothing came of it.

Over the years, the story of our time in Laguna Beach was retold and embellished (the home movie filmed by my mother's youngest sister was screened annually) turning the memory of that place into a happy milestone of my childhood. Now I know that even though my father had a steady job, things were not all that great for them in Laguna Beach. To help make ends meet my mother went to work as a salesgirl in a five-and-dime store. It was quite a step down from the bookkeeping and accounting career she had trained for at the highly respected Katherine Gibbs Secretarial School in Manhattan. It was shameful and embarrassing for a 1940s wife to admit that her husband was unable to support his family and it was something she would never let on about to her parents.

The 3,000-mile separation from family was difficult for my mother, especially after her youngest sister, Patricia, paid us a visit. It's not hard to imagine the impact that visit had on a homesick young Margo or what conflicts it may have stirred up in an already shaky marriage. I do know that in mid-December 1947, two weeks before Christmas, Dod and Margo packed up everything they owned in a car my dad had nicknamed "the yellow peril," and we headed back to 448 Marlboro Road, my maternal grandparents' home in Wood-Ridge, New Jersey.

The major impetus for the trip, I'm sure, was the fact that Margo was once again pregnant and the disheartening circumstance of giving birth so far away from her family was likely more than she was willing to bear.

We arrived in New Jersey just in time for the famous Blizzard of '47, which started on Christmas day and dumped twenty-six inches of snow on New Jersey within forty-eight hours. No doubt, Dod regretted the decision to leave Laguna Beach.

I had just turned three and already I had racked up quite a few adventures; twice, I had crossed the country, once by plane and once by car, met a father I had never known, lived in a city where famous movie stars resided, and returned to New Jersey in the biggest blizzard since 1888. I may have been too young to know it, but the excitement of travel and the thrill of new and challenging exploits had already been implanted in me.

In New Jersey, I was doted on and cared for by my grandparents and aunts, making the difficult transition from the warmth of California to the frigid cold of New Jersey at least tolerable for my pregnant mother. Not so for my father. Having given up his employment as a police officer, which he truly enjoyed, he was now a man with no job, a second child on the way, living with his wife's parents and, in all likelihood, being supported by them. It couldn't have been easy for him. Perhaps he blamed my mother for these unhappy circumstances, which only added to the stress their marriage was already under, or perhaps he tried to hide his resentment. At my young age, I was not yet aware of the growing tension between them.

My first concrete memory came when I was three-and-a-half years old. As expected, it involved my parents. We were still living with my maternal grandparents when on July 12, 1948, the house was filled with a flurry of excitement which culminated in my father whisking my mother out the front door and leaving me behind. I remember the abruptness of their unexplained departure and the sinking feeling that I would never see them again. My father certainly must have come back home at some point, but the rest of the incident was a blur until a week later, when he returned with my mother and a newborn baby, my sister Karen. (The lengthy hospital stay was due to the accepted practice of keeping new mothers confined to one whole week of complete bed rest postpartum.)

My clearest impression of that experience was not about the joyful arrival of my baby sister or any possible feelings of sibling rivalry. Instead, it stamped me with a lasting anxiety about my father leaving and the alarming possibility he might never return. This fear of abandonment by a beloved father figure would recur throughout my childhood and become a significant feature in my life. As an adult, it would manifest and play out in different ways with each of the significant men in my life.

In stark contrast there is another memory, one so ephemeral that I'm never sure if it is factual or imaginary. I can only describe it as a feeling that comes over me when I least expect it – so fleeting that I experience both exhilaration and disappointment in a nano-second – exhilaration at being back in a place of great happiness, and disappointment in not being able to stay long enough to investigate and explore it. This "place" appears to me in a recurring *déjà vu* which can overtake me at any moment, whether I'm in familiar territory, traveling the world, or even looking at a simple photograph. The experience is always triggered by a common feature: a winding staircase made of stone or wood, adorned by lush vegetation and a closed door or gate that beckons to me.

No matter how hard I've tried to locate this memory, the best I can come up with is that it might have been somewhere in Laguna Beach, perhaps along the path we took from the house on Ruby Road to the ocean. Over the years I've been tempted to go back to try and find it, but finally I decided the rediscovery might put an end to this interesting phenomenon which has been with me as long as I can remember and continues to surprise, delight, and puzzle me to this day.

After the birth of my sister, Karen, the memories began to pile up. Dod took a job at Sears & Roebuck selling sewing machines. It was a far cry from the exciting police work he left behind but he had valid credentials for this new position. Part of his time in the Marine Corps was spent as a parachutist. Not only did he have to know how to pack his own chute, he was required to manufacture it as well. I doubt if he ever guessed that learning how to operate a sewing machine would one day become a marketable skill, but it paid the bills.

One afternoon my mother took me and baby sister Karen to Sears to visit our father. I can still see him seated at a sewing machine demonstrating its features to a middle-aged woman customer. On his face, a blank expression, in his eyes, a faraway look. It was a striking picture of a brave Marine reduced to a meaningless, almost female role. That may well be when his problems with alcohol began.

Once we finally moved out of our grandparents' house into our own apartment at 1415 Palisades Avenue, Union City, New Jersey, Dod and Margo were free to regularly engage in volatile confrontations, often fueled by liquor, which threatened their marriage. My maternal grandparents continued to lend us their support, sending us bags of groceries, taking us to Radio City Music Hall, and making sure that Karen and I always had some special holiday outfit. Best of all were the summers we spent at their vacation home on Lake Mohawk in Sparta, New Jersey – the same lake where my parents met.

Returning to that magical spot every summer became the highlight of my life. From the day school let out in June until the start of the new semester in September, my mother, my sister Karen, and I would head off for the lake. My father never came with us, ostensibly because he had to work, but I knew the truth. Dod wasn't there because he and Margo couldn't get along. Other fathers came up on weekends to be with their families, in fact it was the father of one of my friends who taught me to dive and water ski. As much as I appreciated his instruction, it was a weekly reminder of how wrong things were in our family. Karen and I loved our summers in Mohawk, but there was always the underlying sense of how difficult it was for our mother. She had no friends nearby and our grandparents only came up on the weekends. Mom was very alone and would spend her days sitting on the narrow strip of beach watching Karen and me happily splashing in the crystal-clear lake while she read a book or stared off into space, perhaps enjoying the splendid scenery, but more likely thinking about her unhappy life with Dod.

Basically, our mother's parents were providing us with all the niceties our father could not afford. To Dod, this was a slap in the face and any new gift was just the excuse he needed to unleash another tirade against my mother and her family for interfering in our lives. These occurrences became so habitual that by the time I was seven years old, I thought it was my duty to keep their marriage together and to shield my baby sister Karen from their wrath. I pleaded and cajoled and pulled out every "good little girl" trick in the book to lessen their conflicts, but no matter how hard I tried, my world became increasingly unstable.

ON JUNE 25, 1950, THE COLD WAR between Russia and the United States broke out in open conflict in the Asian peninsula of Korea when 75,000 troops from Communist North Korea invaded Western-influenced South

Korea. With the terrifying vision of atomic mushroom clouds still hovering in our minds, home bomb shelters and "duck and cover drills" became part of the American way of life. With the increase of the "Korean Conflict," young men were once again being asked to sacrifice for their country.

As a former Marine, Dod was required to spend five years in the Marine Corps Reserves. Twelve days before the end of his five-year term he received a notice commanding him to report to active duty. There's no doubt that when Dod was called up for duty in the Korean War he was ready to go. In stark contrast, my mother now with two young daughters and no regular income, envisioned herself resuming the unhappy role of "war wife," with real concerns about losing the apartment and moving back in with her parents.

The day of Dod's departure, I stood in New York's cavernous Grand Central Station, alongside my mother, her middle sister, Alice, and my six-foot, handsome "war hero" daddy. Dwarfed by the enormity of the vaulted ceiling, vast foyer, and iconic four-sided clock, we waited for the train that would take Daddy away – again. When the sad moment of parting arrived, there were hugs and kisses all around. As my father stepped onto the sleek silver train, he turned and blew me a kiss. It was as if the kiss hit my heart directly, breaking it in two. I looked up at my mother hoping to share my heartbreak, only to find her engaged in giggling with Aunt Alice – her back to the train – the train that was taking my Daddy away! The message was clear; sadness is not appropriate or appreciated and deep emotions are to be ignored. I gulped down the lump in my throat and never let on how devastated or confused I was. To this day that lump returns at the very thought of that miserable day.

Luckily, this time Dod never left the shores of the West Coast and due to his age and marital status, he was eligible for discharge in about three months. His unexpected return came one afternoon when Margo was in the kitchen making Christmas pies. There was a knock on the door. She told me to answer it. I ran to open the door and found myself in the shadow of my beloved father. "Mom," I screamed, "Daddy's home!" There were genuine tears of relief and an embrace that seemed to go on forever. At that moment, all my fears that my parents wouldn't stay together vanished and I thought we would once again be a real family.

CHAPTER 2

Separation to Reconciliation

1950-1960

The three short months my father spent back in the U.S. Marine Corps must have renewed his sense of direction. On his return home, without consulting my mother Margo, he applied for a job with the New Jersey State Troopers, the police force made famous during the 1935 kidnapping of celebrated aviator Charles Lindberg's infant son. While my mom saw police work as a less than desirable occupation, Dod praised it as a secure means of making a living. His rationale was, "The State of New Jersey will never go bankrupt; therefore, I will always have a job!"

For twenty-six weeks, he traveled the sixty-six-mile trip from Union City to Trenton, New Jersey, to complete his training at the New Jersey Police Academy. The practice at that time was for all new troopers to spend their first year on motorcycles. Dod was a brave marine, but even to him, riding a 1948 Harley Davidson motorcycle in high-speed chases was dangerous and scary as hell. One such event, which he barely survived, gave him nightmares for years. No wonder Margo was not in favor of his career choice.

Like everything my father undertook, he eventually excelled at it. His graduation ceremony took place in the state capitol of Trenton, New Jersey, on a hot, humid, summer day. My mother, my sister and I, along with my maternal grandparents and all my aunts (the McGivney sisters), were in attendance. Dod ranked near, or at the top of his class, and while we watched from a grassy hillside, on a broad field below us, he led a motorcycle parade of all the graduating troopers, weaving in and out of various formations on their monster 1948 Harley Davidson bikes. Only years later would I come to appreciate the amount of skill it took to execute those intricate patterns, on grass, nonetheless. Seeing my father at the front of the pack in his blue trooper uniform, leading all the other men, made me swell with pride and no doubt imprinted on me a lasting image that would greatly influence my life – a handsome, powerful man on a motorcycle – a man who held my heart in his hands.

That day, while we were waiting in line for the ladies' room, one of my very gutsy Irish Catholic aunts announced that since there was no line for the men's room we would use that, and take turns watching the door for each other. I felt a giddy excitement at this seemingly taboo gesture and at the shock of seeing my first urinal. It was a big day for a five-year-old.

BEING A NEW JERSEY STATE trooper meant that my father was assigned to living in what were called "the barracks." Troopers were required to be temporarily stationed in various locations throughout New Jersey. It was not the kind of stationing which would lead a family to move. We were in our three-room apartment, but his schedule was irregular. He would be home for two days, back for one, then off he'd go again. It seemed he was always coming and going so there was never a feeling of permanence to our home life. One afternoon I was playing with a friend, Raymond Ricard, in his next-door apartment. Raymond's father was a merchant marine who traveled the world. On one trip, he brought back stuffed koalas for me and my sister. Raymond had a collection of wonderful toys and that day I picked up a plastic figurine he had on his bedroom shelf. It was an inexpensive item, something you would find in any toy store, but it completely captivated me. It was a miniature motorcycle with a rider outfitted in a state trooper uniform. I became obsessed with having one and wouldn't stop bugging my parents to get me my own motorcycle figure. Days later when my father was leaving on a hunting trip, he bent down for a kiss goodbye and handed me the same exact motorcycle and rider. That little figure became a surrogate for my father, a symbol that I could keep him near me. For years, just seeing that figure gave me a feeling of comfort.

My father's erratic schedule was not conducive to a healthy family lifestyle. I don't know if that's where the temptations started for him or if it was my mother's resentment that caused him to look elsewhere, but during this time there definitely was another woman in the picture (maybe even more than one) and a lot of grown-up strife at home. My mother incessantly grumbled about my father not being around enough. Yet when he was home, they were both miserable and angry and fought constantly.

Much of my elementary school years were spent in what can best be described as a "broken home." I don't know if my parents ever officially separated because any time my father wanted to leave, he would just pick up and stay in the barracks. My mother, my sister, and I lived in a constant state of insecurity, never knowing when or if he was coming back.

This behavior lasted throughout my elementary school years. I was in a Catholic school where nobody else I knew was experiencing anything like this. No one talked about what was going on in their homes, but having visited other families, I did know that the dad was generally around. I was constantly put in the awkward position of having to explain where my missing father was. Making up lies in that strict Catholic environment was frankly too much for a kid to handle. I was building up a storehouse of false narratives and excuses that were taking an emotional toll on me.

Somewhere between the ages of seven and nine, I had this fantasy that if I were present to observe Dod and Margo's behavior, things wouldn't fall apart. I remember being nervous when I was at school about not being at home. I truly felt I was responsible for keeping their marriage together and the only way I thought I could do that was by loving them both equally and not placing blame on either one of them. In contrast, my sister, being younger, sided with my mother and I could see that having to reject our father was causing her a lot of pain. I felt I needed to make her understand that it wasn't any one person's fault. I set out a three-fold game plan for myself; I would be equally good to mom and dad, I would save their marriage, and I would protect my sister from the mayhem.

Why a nine-year-old child would take on this kind of burden, I will never know — but that's what I did.

DESPITE HOW DIFFICULT things were at home, Dod was thriving in the New Jersey troopers. He eventually became an instructor who taught the trainees everything from better driving skills to the correct handling of firearms.

Sometimes he would take me and Karen with him for a weekend to Sea Girt, New Jersey to an old army base where he taught. I can remember overhearing him talking to a woman on the phone saying, "No, you're not going to meet my kids." I clearly understood the implications of that conversation and knew instinctively it was something I would never mention to my mother.

When I became a teenager, things got worse. Karen and I began spending every Saturday afternoon with our father. He would take us bowling or to some other "fun activity," but when he dropped us off at home inevitably my sister and I would be told to stay outside because Dod and Margo "had some things to talk over." Karen and I would stay out on the stoop and distract ourselves by singing some new popular song or practicing one of the cheerleading moves that I was working on at school, pretending we didn't hear the horrible screaming match going on inside our apartment.

I don't know how physical these battles became, but I do remember overhearing my mother on the phone telling her father that Dod had "spanked" her. It was shocking to me — not only that he had struck her, but that she would tell her father about it. I realized the family secrets I tried so hard to hide, were already out in the open and I felt embarrassed and ashamed.

While, on one hand, I was going through this family turmoil, on the other hand, my life was beginning to unfold in new and hopeful ways. I discovered I had a talent for drawing which brought me endless hours of pleasure. As far back as elementary school I had an ability to perfectly render popular cartoon characters like Mickey Mouse and Donald Duck. My father had the same artistic ability and he produced all kinds of wonderful pencil drawings mostly of shapely pinup girls similar to the famed drawings of George Petty and Alberto Vargas, which graced the pages of *Esquire* and other slick magazines in the 1940s. I liked the fact that I had inherited this gift from my father, even though my mother never expressed any approval of either my creative endeavors or my father's.

In my teens, I graduated to copying the fashion drawings in the *New York Times* Sunday edition where they would show these wonderful images of women wearing the latest fashions. The figures were tall and graceful, highly stylized, and elegant. I would spend my Sunday afternoons lost in the pleasure of meticulously recreating them.

It was my father who appreciated my artistic talents and even took the time to teach me that in a normal drawing of a human being, there are what he called "seven heads," meaning that proportionately the height of the figure would be seven times the head size, but in fashion it was always eight heads, which accounted for their elongated look. I was developing a real love of learning and I remember thinking what a wonderful piece of "inside information" for him to give me. It was like a gift from one artist to another.

My father was happy to instruct me on the rules of drawing and when I was about sixteen I asked him, "Do you think I should go to the Fashion Institute?" He promptly replied, "That's a man's world; you'll never make it, so don't even think about doing that." I wasn't thinking about how to make fashion. I just knew that I could copy these drawings and it might be a place where I could improve my drawing skills. But right then and there, he crossed that world off my list. I worshipped my father and I believed he wasn't trying to dismiss my talent; he was just being realistic about my prospects. He knew there were limited choices for women. You could be a teacher or a librarian, or a nurse or a secretary – maybe an airline stewardess. But not a fashion artist. I thought he was right, mainly because I had never seen a woman in any other kind of role. I allowed my father to squash my ambitions because I believed that "Father Knows Best."

Layered on top of all that was my mother saying to me more than once, "You need to do something just in case." To me, the "just in case," meant that at some point in my life I would be without a man, through divorce or through death, and I would have to pick up the pieces and have something to fall back on, the way she had done with her secretarial training.

During these difficult years with my father, she took a job in the accounting department of Sears & Roebuck. While she constantly complained about having to work, it was obvious that she enjoyed it immensely. It was where she had friends and financial security and it gave her a sense of self-respect. It was clear to me that in her eyes, my artistic talents were a mere frivolity and I needed to prepare for a real job; one that paid good money. I took my parents' concerns to heart and stored my artistic talents away in a place marked "for amusement only."

WHEN I WAS IN THE SEVENTH grade in Catholic school, I was the vice president of the Vocation Club, which offered an opportunity for girls to explore different career choices. I was feeling a lot of pressure at school from the nuns who were not so subtly trying to enlist us into their chosen way of life. They repeatedly expressed their belief that while being married was the right thing for a good Catholic girl to do, it was far below being a nun in the Catholic Church. One day I came home from school and said, "I think what I might want to be is a nun." My mother was ironing, with her back to me and without missing a beat, she said, "Over my dead body." In some strange way, that was comforting. I wasn't truly committed to becoming a nun. I just was testing out the idea and her response made me feel she had my back on this one and I didn't have to ever consider it again.

THE ONE STEADY MALE FIGURE in my life was my maternal grandfather, Grandpa McGivney. He was short and round with chubby fingers, which surprisingly, were amazingly dexterous. He was an enormously talented guy; not only did he play the drums, but he was an ace pool player and an accomplished baton twirler, a skill he passed on to me. One day when I was about twelve, I was sitting on Grandpa McGiveny's lap discussing my future and he said to me, "How about being a lawyer? Or an architect?" I actually scoffed at his outlandish suggestions. I was already brainwashed about what women could or couldn't do, but I know that what he said made a lasting impression on me. Perhaps he saw something in me that I didn't see in myself.

With the limited career options for girls in mind I volunteered at the Hoboken Hospital as a Candy Striper – one of those smiling young girls who float through hospitals in striped uniforms trying to bring joy into the lives of unhappy patients. I enjoyed the work and had a knack for it. The well-ordered hospital regimen was comfortable for me, reminiscent of the kind of training my sister and I had received from our Marine Drill Sargent father, who taught us to make a bed so tight you could bounce a quarter on it.

～～⁓

REGIMENTATION AND DISCIPLINE were part of my everyday life, especially at St. Michael's Catholic High School. I was a good student and loved learning. Acquiring knowledge gave me a feeling of competency, but like all teenagers I wanted to be a part of the in-crowd. Most of the girls I admired were cheerleaders and I thought cheerleading could be my entrée into their elite clique. I signed up to try out for the squad and could already picture myself in the cute letterman sweater and short skirt they wore to perform their energetic pom-pom routines. My parents had taught me that the keys to success were dedication, determination, and hard work. I threw myself headlong into my pursuit, faithfully attending every practice session and working on my moves at home in front of a mirror or with my sister Karen. Being a cheerleader was all I dreamed of and I became focused, laser-like, on my objective.

Three other girls I had known since grammar school were also trying out to become cheerleaders and we bonded even closer in our hopes of making the team together. Then finally, the long-anticipated day came for the tryouts. After weeks of hard work and striving, the selections were posted – all of my friends made the team – I did not. I was devastated. I had pinned so much hope on this. My entire social standing in St. Michael's High School depended on it, and now I was nothing – nobody. I would never be accepted into the privileged circle. I went home heartbroken and sobbed my eyes out. My mother tried to comfort me as best she could, but my grief was inconsolable. I had been rejected and I had no reservoir of self-esteem to help me cope. Instead, I hunkered down to lick my wounds and prayed for a way to survive this huge disappointment.

For days, I pondered what had gone wrong. What could I have done differently? How could I change this bleak outcome? Slowly I began to see the bigger picture. Truthfully, there were only so many spots available and many more applicants than openings on the team. Maybe there was some element of social snobbery involved, but I didn't want to dwell on that; instead, I needed to find a way to make myself whole again. Then it came to me – there were other components to the half-time spectacle at the football games besides the cheerleaders; there was the marching band, the drum majorettes and the baton twirlers! Grandpa McGiveny's skill which he had passed on to me was about to pay off.

I gathered myself together, headed into the office of the coach in charge of the baton twirling team and offered myself as a prime candidate. "I already know how to twirl so you won't have to teach me anything; in fact, I can help the other girls who are just learning." It worked like a charm. Suddenly, I was a valued member of a team. It may not have been the cheerleading squad, but truthfully, our uniforms were much classier; military style, like West Point cadets, with tall, peaked caps, jackets with shiny buttons and gold braid across the chest, and white boots with tassels. Our squad had only ten members as opposed to the nearly thirty girls in the cheerleading squad. I was proud to be a part of this team and eagerly looked forward to the coming semester where we were scheduled to participate in a local parade, lead the football team onto the field and perform in the half-time extravaganza.

It was my junior year at St. Michael's High and I was feeling much better about myself. We were practicing for the opening game of the season and already I was imagining myself in my spiffy looking uniform, perfectly executing my high baton throws while my family and friends watched in awe from the stands.

One evening I came home from practice to find Dod in our kitchen with Margo. That was unusual as he had been mostly staying away. They both looked very serious. Before I could ask Karen what was going on, Dod came in and said, "Girls come in the kitchen. Mom and I want to talk to you." I could see he was crying and the tone of his voice clutched at my heart. My first thought was, "This is it… the end. They're finally going to make the Big D happen." As they sat us down at the kitchen table I could see my mother was weepy too. My father started talking in a calm and measured voice, unlike how he'd spoken for a long time.

"I've been offered this job at Princeton University where I've been asked to create a security department on campus. I asked Mom if she would consider all of us going there, and she said yes." It took me a minute to process the full impact of this information. Essentially it meant that my parents were getting back together. The reconciliation that I had prayed so hard for was about to come true. Instead of being thankful, my immediate reaction was the realization that my life was being upended and all the plans I had made, including my imminent baton twirling performance, were about to come to a screeching halt. Now it was my turn to cry. I remember saying something like, "I worked hard at doing this; this is my life and now you're going to take it all away, just like that?"

Obviously, something I said moved them. In an unusual show of solidarity, they sat down with the counselor at St. Michael's and arranged for me to come back in the Fall and perform my baton twirling routine at the opening game which I did to perfection, with my parents and sister sitting in the stands. When the game was over, we got in the car, drove to Princeton, New Jersey, and never looked back.

CHAPTER 3

Dodwell's Daughter

1960-1964

The minute I saw Princeton High School, I was in love. Architecturally, it looked exactly like Princeton University – gothic and beautiful. I had come from a Catholic high school where gym class was a joke because God forbid girls sweat! We didn't have real gyms. We didn't have lockers; we didn't even wear proper gym clothes. We had to wear culottes with stockings. To this day I don't know what that was about.

At Catholic school, the nuns moved from one classroom to another while the students stayed in the same place. At Princeton High, the students moved from classroom to classroom while the teachers stayed in place. To me this was a novel concept. There was a real gym with lockers and a home economics class and a shop class. It was amazing! This was an actual high school, like one you'd see in a Hollywood movie. I could barely contain myself. My brain was working overtime, imagining the wonderful things that might take place in this magical setting.

On my first day at Princeton High, something happened that I will never forget. I was sitting down with my mother and the school counselor to discuss what classes I would be assigned to. The counselor looked over my academic records and said, "We'll send Linda to this English class and this math class and I think this art class would be good for her." My heart skipped a beat. At St. Michael's I had gotten straight A's in art class, which basically meant learning how to do stuff with Popsicle sticks. Fortunately, the counselor didn't know that. I quickly glanced at my mother fearing she would voice an objection, but she said nothing. Nor did I. I don't remember anything else that took place at that meeting. My brain was fixated on replaying the words, "I think this art class would be good for her." It was like a magic door was being opened and I was invited to enter where previously I had been forbidden to go. Someone had acknowledged my interest… had acknowledged me.

The first day I entered art class my heart was racing with excitement. It was unlike any classroom I had ever been in. Easels and jars of paint were stacked along one wall and all manner of brushes and pencils were lined up in neatly arranged containers. "Wow!" I thought, "This is a real art class." The teacher, Mr. Stetzin, put me in the first row at a kind of desk I'd never seen before – an art desk with an extra-large surface, big enough to hold a drawing pad. Everything here was unique and special.

My best buddies in the class were a talented young boy named John Lithgow and a girl named Nancy Reinheimer, an oboe player who would become my best friend. Like me, they had both come into the class in October, a month later than everyone else. My late arrival was because of my twirling performance but theirs was because of their fathers' work schedules. Both of their fathers, like mine, worked at Princeton where classes started in October. John's father ran the McCarter Theatre department and Nancy's father taught in the music department. Due to our delayed arrivals, we three acquired a status as "newcomers" which in turn led to our bond of friendship.

John and his family lived upstairs from us in the Hibben Apartments on the shore of Lake Carnegie and we often rode to school together. My great admiration for John's talent came when he tacked up a roll of butcher paper the width of the back wall of the art room and free hand drew a panoramic family picnic scene. My work had all been copying other people's work and I was astounded at his imaginative abilities which proved to be prodigious as he moved from art into acting and eventually became a famous stage, TV, and movie actor. (My one claim to fame – I knew John Lithgow when.)

For our very first art assignment, Mr. Stetzin brought in a puppy and said, "Today I want you to do five drawings of this puppy." My first reaction was total panic, "How were we supposed to draw a moving target?" Much to my surprise, I pulled it off well. By the end of the class, I knew I was in the right place.

～～〜

ON THE HOME FRONT, things were a lot better. Dod had a well-paying job that brought him recognition and satisfaction. Margo loved bragging about his success, especially to her sister Pat, whose husband had become a VP at some Wall Street firm. She never let Margo forget it. Before long, Margo too had found employment at Princeton University, where her bookkeeping skills landed her a job in the controller's office. At last, my parents were able to enjoy a marriage that wasn't fraught with anger and frustration. The alcohol problem that had plagued my father wasn't rearing its ugly head as often and I was flourishing in these new and happier surroundings.

Unfortunately, my sister Karen had a difficult transition. Ever since kindergarten up through the sixth grade, she had been quite the popular girl and the hub of a really delightful group of friends. Wrenching her away from this comfort was more than she could bear. Her Princeton elementary school arrival in October was like mine, a month later than the other students. Without the safety blanket of the close friendships she had enjoyed in Union City, she became one miserable youngster. And she let everyone know it. Dod's attitude was, "She'll adapt eventually; stop giving in to her." Margo being a mom did the opposite, catering to her every whim. For the first time, I felt that life was going smoothly and here was Karen causing all kinds of chaos. It seemed like things were never going to be peaceful in our household. Fortunately, in time everything got resolved. Once Princeton became home, Union City faded into memory, but it took the whole of seventh grade for my sister to find her way.

Karen and I were three-and-a-half years apart in age but we were four years apart in school years. That allowed Karen to have her Princeton High

School years to herself without an elder sister reigning over her. She was free to be the star of her own universe and she thrived at Princeton High as much as I did.

As a youngster in Catholic school I had been taught never to go into a Protestant church, let alone hang out there. Now, with all my new friends at Princeton High, that's exactly what I was doing, and I was I enjoying it! Much to my delight it was a great opportunity to get to know previously forbidden Protestants – especially Protestant boys.

Luckily for me, shortly after we moved to Princeton, another Linda, Linda McBride, who lived across the street, took me under her wing. I was a nerdy Catholic girl with funky, horrible sneakers, skirts of the wrong length and a head of hair that was the disastrous result of a Toni Home Permanent. Linda transformed my hairdo with these crazy looking things called rollers, got me to shorten my skirts, and basically changed my look. Once she did this makeover, I felt completely different and realized for the first time I was actually getting noticed by boys. Previously, when I had walked through the campus to my dad's office, my appearance hadn't caused a ripple among the 3,000 all-male student body. As soon as Linda worked her magic on me, the opposite happened. Suddenly I was turning heads on the Princeton campus.

The other remarkable consequence of Linda McBride's friendship was a seemingly automatic membership into an elite lunch group comprised of senior boys and junior girls who had their own special table in the lunchroom. It was a privilege for any girl to be invited to sit at their table, especially somebody who was brand new to the school. It almost made up for the way I had been treated by the snobby cheerleader clique at St. Michael's.

At Princeton High, this "special group" was in charge of playing music in the lunchroom and even though we weren't permitted to get up and dance, we would dance sitting down; shaking our bodies and clapping our hands while George "Sonny" Russo, one of the Junior boys who had a vast collection of 45 rpms, would spin our favorites and hold court like a rock 'n' roll king. We were the kids who would smoke out in the smoking area off the cafeteria and we each had a "church key," a run-of-the-mill beer can opener painted gold worn on a chain around the neck for all to see which signified we were part of this "in-crowd." It was a memorable junior year.

When our senior year rolled around, all our male friends from the previous semester had graduated. We girls looked at the new crop of senior boys, who the previous year had been like brothers to us, and it didn't seem plausible to actually have a romantic interest in any of them.

I had one other classmate, Lucille Toto, whose dad was a professor at Princeton. Lucille and I decided to explore the idea of dating some of the college guys from Princeton. I already knew it would make me a pariah with the high school boys who always put down the college guys with a rivalry referred to as "town vs gown." Even so, I started to hang out on the college campus. My dad's job made that easy for me to do.

Princeton University had a lot of sports teams and as Head of Security, my dad attended all the hockey games, football and basketball games, and endless sporting events that were an important part of campus life. I would tag along with my dad; just to hang out, be around the scene. It didn't take long for guys to know that I was Dodwell's daughter, which was kind of a double-edged sword, because there was always the question, "How close do you want to get to security?" I think my dad liked that. There was this sort of hands-off policy surrounding me so that, in a sense, I was protected.

I graduated from Princeton High School in 1962 and much to the chagrin of my mother, I immediately enrolled in the Ann May School of Nursing. My mother not so secretly hoped I would follow her into a secretarial career. She couldn't fathom my desire to go into nursing. I would come home with all these heart-pounding stories about surgical procedures and dramatic life-and-death scenarios which my father loved to hear about and my mother fairly bristled at. "How can you do that?" she questioned. "I don't know," I replied, "it makes sense to me, and I'm good at it." And I was good at it. I must admit there was another aspect that I enjoyed; going into nursing was the first time I openly rejected my mother's plans for me. It was the start of my rebellion and it was empowering.

The nursing school and the hospital we worked at, Fitkin Memorial Hospital (now Jersey Shore Medical), were in Neptune, New Jersey, a coastal city bordering to the west of Asbury Park, a one-hour drive from Princeton. I and another girl, Joan Lackey, who had also chosen nursing, were driven back and forth weekly by our fathers who shared the driving duties. One weekend when Joan's father was driving, we were involved in an auto accident. I sustained a broken ankle. Out of that came a nice insurance package. In my travels, back and forth to school, I had noticed this cute convertible Volkswagen bug on the side of the road with a FOR SALE sign on it. My insurance money exactly covered the cost. I casually mentioned my sighting of the "perfect car" to mom and dad, never expecting anything to come of it. The following weekend there were the keys for me to find in my bedroom! My initial buzz was quelled when mom and dad determined I needed more than one weekend of driving practice… it was, after all, a stick shift, not an automatic transmission. Little did they realize I could see right through them – they eventually confessed – they wanted time for themselves to drive this cute bug of a car to show to all their friends in town.

For two weekends, Dod, the New Jersey State Trooper Driving Instructor, took me to the empty parking lot of the nearby deserted shopping mall and with the aid of cigarette after cigarette, sat next to me, barely surviving the experience, as I ground gear after gear. Finally, I got the hang of it and was sent off on my own, free of dad's chauffeuring service. Now, with my own car, I became even more admired on campus. At that time Princeton was an all-male university and none of the 3,000 male students was allowed to have a car on campus or drive one within a one-hundred-mile radius.

This "auto-free" campus restriction started back in the early 1930s when cars were becoming very popular and Princeton had a number of campus casualties due to drunk driving. One day, the Princeton administrators sat down with the students and gave them a choice: "You can have liquor on campus, but no driving, or you can have driving but no liquor." It's easy to guess what they voted for. Now, only certain cars were waved in at the campus security kiosks. Being Dodwell's daughter, I was one of the few cleared to pass. That made me even more popular with the boys.

My plan to date a few Princeton University guys worked out fine. Actually, I went through a series of fellas. They were all very wholesome, fun adventures. I dated a hockey player, a swimmer, went camping with one fellow, Jim – God he was cute! I enjoyed some typical collegiate romances; a rush of excitement followed by terrible disappointment, but I took it all in stride. Some of my admirers got to meet my parents. I always felt it was brave of these young men to stand the test as to whether or not they could handle being around Mr. Dodwell. He still had that serious, tough Marine look about him and he wasn't easily won over.

There was one student Dod did take a shine to. He wasn't one of the boys I had been dating; this was a boy he had learned about from the coach of the freshmen football team. His name was Larry Stupski, a kid from a blue-collar background in Jacksonville, Florida, who excelled at everything he did. At Terry Parker High, in Jacksonville, he had been vale-dictorian, captain of the football team, captain of the basketball team, on the student senate and class president. He was accepted by every school he applied to, including all the military academies. His football coach talked him into taking the Princeton acceptance. Even though it cost a lot of money, Larry managed it with a scholarship and a full-time job in the dining hall. Dod was very impressed with this boy. Perhaps he saw Larry as the son he never had even though their first encounter was under questionable circumstances.

No matter how smart college boys are, they're still boys and can do some really stupid things. One night, Larry and a couple of his football teammates decided to take a big Stillson wrench to the fire hydrant on Nassau Street, the main street of Princeton. The geyser they launched was the talk of the town, on and off campus. Their peers secretly admired these mischief-makers and encouraged them to repeat their crime. They man-aged to get away with it a couple of times. On their third try the local cops, along with the Princeton campus police, known as Proctors, were waiting for them. At the first sound of the bullhorn and the flashing red lights, the boys scattered. Larry made the mistake of ducking into a dead-end street. When he turned around, he was trapped. He had the wrench in his hand and the policeman had a gun in his. Larry was arrested and thrown in jail. It was a sobering moment. The university sent my dad to bail him out. It was part of an unwritten agreement between town and gown.

I had never met the infamous Larry Stupski, but I'd heard a lot about him. One afternoon on a reunion weekend, I was hanging out in my dad's office and in walks this six-foot-tall, curly haired blonde guy, very tanned, muscular, with a great smile and bright eyes. It was Larry Stupski. His freshman spring semester was over, but he had stayed behind in order to earn some money. Larry had been assigned to manage the 50th Class Reunion and needed to secure the reunion's cash in my dad's safe. My instant reaction was, "Hmmm, isn't he handsome!" He must have formed a favorable opinion of me as well because when he finished his business, instead of leaving, he found some excuse to hang out in the office doorway, waiting for my father to introduce us. I thought that was unlikely to happen because my father had informed me soon after we moved to Princeton, that he wanted it to be perfectly clear he, "…wasn't going to be a dating service for me with the young Princeton boys." He had, "…a professional reputation to uphold!" In other words, in the dating department, I would be on my own. When it became uncomfortably clear that Larry wasn't going to leave until Dod introduced us, he grudgingly said, "This is my daughter Linda." Larry flashed that great smile and reached out his hand, "Larry Stupski."

I admired Larry's persistence and could see that he wasn't at all intimidated by Dod. When I got up to leave, he offered to walk me home. It was a long walk, and we took it slow chatting casually and getting to know each other. In a very straightforward way he said, "I'd like to ask you out, but I'm busy this weekend." He must have sensed my disappointment and quickly explained that because he needed to earn some extra money, he'd signed up for a psychology test requiring him to be isolated in a soundproof room for a whole weekend. That seemed a bit drastic to me, but as I would soon learn, Larry was a scrambler when it came to earning money. The weekend came and went and the minute the test was over he went straight to a phone booth and called me which of course impressed the heck out me. It didn't take long to figure out that we were clicking on so many different levels that we didn't even want to think about dating other people. The year was 1964, we were both barely out of our teens, but my parents loved him, I loved him, and he loved me. I found it a bit ironic that the only Princeton guy my dad introduced me to was the man I wanted to spend the rest of my life with.

CHAPTER 4

Nurse to Elopement

1965-1967

As much as I missed being with Larry during the week, I must admit, I loved nursing school. There were only thirty students in the class. It was an old-fashioned, three-year diploma program. Not just book learning, but practical knowledge. There weren't too many days that we didn't actually go on the hospital floor and perform the skills we were being taught in the classroom. We lived in the hospital, in the nurses' dorm, with real nurses' furniture. Nothing glamorous.

At first, I thought I might have a problem getting into the nursing program, but I later learned that pretty much any Catholic girl who applied got in. They liked the Catholic girls because they had discipline and fealty. The three-year program was very rigorous and went year-round with no summers off. We were trained in every aspect of hospital work. Some courses took one month, some three months. There was even a three-month period where we worked with mentally ill patients on the Monmouth Hospital campus and lived in dorms they provided. No matter what the circumstances, I never felt out of my league or overwhelmed, and I managed to get good grades. I even got to use a bit of my art skills. In this small class of nurses, one other girl, Loretta, was also an artist. We were assigned to come up with some drawings for the yearbook, which we did. I got a real kick out of seeing my work published.

In August 1965, at the graduation ceremony, Larry sat alongside my parents in the audience as I received my diploma. I could see them all grinning proudly. It was one of the happiest days of my life...so far.

Soon after graduating, I was hired at St. Barnabas, a new hospital in Livingston, New Jersey. I wanted to be on the exciting side of nursing – the emergency room. But getting a spot in the ER was always impossible; everybody wanted it. I had to settle for the surgery department, which was far more tedious and often meant standing in one spot for hours. I was pretty miserable from day one. I did a fine job being a surgical nurse. I never doubted my ability. I knew what I was doing. At twenty-one years old, I was confident; I just didn't like the work in surgery that much and in truth I didn't like being so far away from Larry. He was in his junior year at Princeton.

I was living in a garden apartment in Livingston with two other girls from Fitkin. On the night of my twenty-first birthday, my grandparents planned to take me out to dinner. I came home so tired from standing on my feet all day I thought I would take off my sensible white shoes and white stockings and soak my poor feet under the tub faucet. Unfortunately, the water came out scalding hot and burned a large patch of skin off my right leg. I watched it go down the drain. The pain was incredible. Neither of my roommates was home, but a fellow nurse whisked me over to the ER, conveniently just across the road, where I had to endure a most painful Phisohex scrub to hopefully remove any and all bacteria. Over the next few days, as I lay at home recuperating, I decided I would move back to Princeton to be with Larry and find a job in a hospital there.

My parents were not too pleased when I asked if I could move back in with them, but they never said no. Larry, who had another year to go before graduation, was ecstatic. I quickly found a job at the Princeton Hospital working on the main floor. Because of my three years of training, I earned the title of Registered Nurse. I was an RN, which gave me seniority over the handful of practical nurses – a designation that required less education and reduced responsibilities. I dove into the work, unaware that my presence was ruffling some feathers. After I'd been there for a while, the head nurse took me aside because it became obvious to her that I was being shunned by the practical nurses who had come to her to complain. I didn't have any problem with them, and I didn't understand why they had a problem with me. The head nurse clued me in, "The problem is you never ask them for help. And you never come to them for anything." She was right, I didn't. I was confident that I could do everything I was asked to do. They were a group of African-American practical nurses who had been working together before I came along and it never dawned on me they were feeling excluded. Once my eyes were opened I took her advice and turned my attitude around. It was an important lesson for me. After that it was more of a team effort and we all actually became very close.

One day I learned that if I was willing to do the evening shift, I could become a head nurse, share the job with another head nurse, and the two of us could work out our schedule any way we liked, including having alternate weekends off. So that's what I did. We had a super situation. We were in charge of fifty-six patients – medical, surgical, and psychiatric. There was one head nurse (me) and an aide. Sometimes I had a practical nurse as well, if I was lucky. My evening schedule started at 3 p.m. and ended at 11 p.m.; just about the time Larry was finished studying. We'd meet up on campus and go to a party afterwards or do something fun. When you're twenty-one, that kind of ridiculous schedule is nothing. In fact, it was perfect for both of us.

Another reason I liked the evening shift was because I had a lot of visitors to help me out with the med/surg/psych patients. During the day, it was constantly busy; all kinds of craziness going on, lots of doctors in and out of surgery; patients being rolled on gurneys, anxious visitors asking endless questions. Around 3 p.m., it was a lot calmer. The rest of the departments were pretty much shut down. Everyone was starting to settle in for the night and you had more control over the floor. I was in charge of IVs and meds, and I had an aide who would go around and make sure the beds were taken care of. The visiting relatives didn't realize they were helping, but they would be kind of baby-sitting, so you could juggle the work without any problem.

It all ran smoothly, until one night when the practical nurse on duty nearly hung the wrong blood type for one of the patients. Somewhere along the line she had been told that she had a right to do that job. As a practical nurse, she did not. I caught her error just in time. That slip could have killed the patient. I remember thinking if that had happened, I would have been the one to lose my license.

Very quickly I started to look for another option. Across the parking lot was an L-shaped building that housed fifteen doctors: internists, surgeons, dermatologists, and three OB/GYN's. As a summer job between junior and senior year in high school, I had worked there as an all-around 'gopher' because one of the OB/GYN docs happened to be a high school classmate of Dod's. Now, a nurse who worked there for five internists was moving to New Haven, Connecticut, and needed someone to replace her. She said, "Maybe you'd like this job. You'll have Sundays and Mondays off, and you'll just work eight hours a day." I jumped at the chance.

Around the time I got the new job, Larry got the good news that he had been accepted to Yale Law School. He was still several months away from graduating from Princeton, but I think we both had it in our minds that eventually, at some point we would be moving to New Haven, Connecticut, most likely as a married couple.

IN THE SUMMER OF 1966, Larry and I were invited to visit one of his college roommates at his family home, which sat on a beautiful bay in Maryland. It was a spectacular morning and Larry and I were wading, ankle deep on the shoreline, hoping to catch some of the famed Maryland crabs that skittered along the damp sand. We were both dressed in our summer clothes, shorts and T shirts, looking tan and beautiful. We were having a great time; laughing at our bungled attempts at crabbing or cheering each other on when we managed to grab one of the fast-moving creatures. Out of the blue, Larry turned to me and asked, "Will you marry me?" Without a moment's hesitation I said, "Yes."

There was no getting down on one knee, no ring, none of that. It was the mid-sixties; ceremony and traditions were becoming a thing of the past. But I was still old-fashioned enough to know that my desire to make it official involved a ring. Larry found that difficult to accept. He was poor. He was on scholarship. He spent a lot of time scrounging for extra jobs. He never had cash to throw around. I understood all that, but the ring was important to me.

Reluctant as he was to make the financial commitment, he let me steer him into a jewelry store on Nassau Street in Princeton and we came out with an antique ring which I loved. It was a simple diamond with filigree on the side and the original owner's initials engraved on the inner band. It cost the whopping sum of $125, but it was priceless to me – a sign of our commitment to one another. Once there was a ring on my finger, I was ready to make the announcement to my family. Needless to say, both my mother and father were thrilled.

Dod and Margo were huge sports fans. In his senior year, Larry was playing lacrosse and football. He was a defensive end, a position that never gets to be the hero until one memorable game in which Larry intercepted the ball and scored the winning touchdown. My mother was so excited she jumped up, pointed to me and blurted out to everyone in the stands, "She's engaged to him! She's engaged to him."

The next day the *New York Times* reported:

> "*Stupski's 40-Yard Run With Blocked Punt Wins for Tigers, Princeton Defeats Yale, 13-7, By Scoring in Final Minutes.*"

Amazingly, the following week he did the same thing in the game against Harvard, which, of course, prompted a similar reaction from Mom. I must admit, while I may have been a bit embarrassed by her outburst, I was pretty damn proud. It was a big deal. Larry and those two games, against Yale and Harvard, are both memorialized in the Princeton archives.

MY MOTHER DOVE HEADLONG into planning our wedding which was scheduled for the weekend after Larry's graduation. In no time, she was totally crazed about who to invite. There was this whole thing going on about inviting people I didn't even know and other people complaining about who was being invited and who wasn't. It led to all kinds of upheaval and conflict. I was getting really worn down by all the family squabbles.

In December, Larry and I went to Florida to visit his family. While we were there, he got it into his head that we should elope. With all the chaos that was going on at home, elopement sounded like a really good idea to me. Plus, my sister Karen was getting ready to start college and I thought whatever money my parents would be spending on a wedding would be better off going to her education. In Florida, Larry and I snuck away from his family one afternoon and drove hour after hour looking for a justice of the peace or some sort of government official who would marry us. As it turned out, it was a fruitless adventure because it was smack dab in the middle of the Christmas-New Year holiday week and everything was closed. But once we'd made our minds up to elope, we decided we would do it as soon as we got back to Princeton.

I spent the next two weeks researching the best way to get married. We had decided to keep it a secret for a while so I had to find someplace that was not too far away from Princeton so that we could do it and get back to our routines in one day. What I came up with was Elkton, Maryland, famous, or infamous, for being the elopement center of the East Coast. Elkton was the one place locally where you didn't have to get the three-day blood test for syphilis and gonorrhea which most states required in order to marry. Twelve minutes and a few dollars were all you needed. You could basically just drive there, take your pick of any one of the many chapels on East Main Street and sign on the dotted line. After a brief ceremony, you'd officially be married. That sounded perfect to us.

I went out and bought a white suit and talked my sister into coming along as my maid of honor. Larry bought me a wedding ring that cost $14

— a plain band with a bit of beading on both sides. It fit my needs perfectly and it was within his limited budget.

There were only two married student couples in all of Princeton — Dave and Kathy Martin and Pete and Penny Savage. The husbands being fellow footballers were close friends of ours. Pete was the captain of the team. It seemed only natural that one of the couples supply the best man, Dave, and the other hold down the fort for the reception at their apartment when we returned.

Because Karen and I were both still living at home with our parents, we gave them some lame excuse about what we were up to and off we went. It was snowing hard and it had to have been at least a three- or four-hour drive to Elkton. We finally arrived and found an appropriately plain chapel. I in my white suit and Larry in his one good jacket stood impatiently listening to the woman performing the ceremony as she poured her effusive and unnecessary prayers on us. I remember being very fidgety and annoyed as she tried her best to turn our quickie wedding into a religious event. Larry with his eyes cast down, sent me a signal to chill – "It's not that big of a deal." It was to me. Catholic school had given me all the religion I could handle. The whole wedding must have taken thirty minutes. We got back in the car turned around and headed straight back to New Jersey where Larry and I snuck off to his dorm room for our "honeymoon."

My sister traveled back home on the bus and provoked my mother's rage when she called home and asked to be picked up at the bus station. Margo, an avid Princeton basketball fan, was most perturbed at having her TV game interrupted in the fourth quarter. Poor Karen — she not only had to endure keeping a secret, she had to wait at the local bus stop in the snowstorm until Mom was good and ready to pick her up. I came home to my parents' house later that evening as if nothing had happened.

OF COURSE, I WAS DYING to tell everybody, but Larry and I decided that we couldn't spring it on anyone until we had a place to live. One of the JV football trainers was a local real estate mogul with little apartments everywhere. He was able to steer us towards a tiny off-campus "one room with a kitchen," that was a short walk to campus. It was affordable because I had my nursing job. So, now we were married and had our first place. We were just about ready to tell the world what we'd done.

I'd been taking my wedding ring on and off, particularly when I knew we were going to be around family and friends, until one night when I felt it was time to break the news. Princeton doesn't have fraternities; they have something called eating clubs where you don't actually live, but where you do all your socializing and have meals. Larry was a member of what was called the "Cottage Club." One night we were headed to Cottage for dinner and I decided to wear my wedding band. Right away people started to notice and asked the obvious question, "Did you two tie the knot?" The news spread through the club like wildfire. It became clear that we had to get to my parents quickly because my father was popular among the students and it wouldn't have been unusual for some tipsy club member to call my dad and say, "Congratulations on the marriage."

We decided to head straight over to my parents' apartment. Mom, Dod, my sister, and her boyfriend, Jeff, were just sitting down to dinner. They welcomed us, pulled up a pair of chairs and Larry and I sat down. Right away there was this awkward feeling in the air. My sister was acting weird and my dad was looking at us strangely. Finally, he said, "Is there something you want to tell us?" I gulped and looked at Larry who sucked in a big breath and said, "Well, yeah, we're here to tell you, we got married on January 28th. My father became silent but my mother stood straight up, throwing her hands in the air saying, "I knew it, I knew it, I knew it."

It turns out that because I had stopped being enthusiastic about looking for gowns and places to have the wedding, she became suspicious. I never did know if she was upset because we didn't have the big wedding or if my dad felt he got robbed of walking me down the aisle. They never expressed any of that to me. They were just so happy that Larry was their son-in-law that nothing else mattered. I would often say to people, "They like him better than me." He really was the son they had always wished for.

~~∽

IMAGINE OUR SHOCK when the university heads informed us that Larry had failed to get permission to get married. The penalty on the books was expulsion! Luckily, the Dodwells were liked and respected so the excitement quickly died down, much to our relief.

CHAPTER 5

Honeymoon Interrupted

1967-1969

In this one-room studio apartment with a tiny kitchen and a fold-out couch that turned into a double bed, Larry and I were probably the happiest we would ever be. We bought a few pots and pans and started our life together. In the first week of our marriage Larry had to finish his senior thesis. Princeton was one of the rare undergraduate schools that required a thesis to graduate. We spent hours, days, weeks, at the engineering quad where they had an early IBM computer. It was bigger than a house. This was the day of IBM punch cards and everything you wanted the computer to do had to be typed out on these elongated cards. You'd put them into this machine, one box at a time, and hours later it would produce yards and yards of printouts of the requested research calculations. It was extremely time consuming and laborious. The cards had to be inserted in a specific order and if any of them got mixed up your project was dead. I remember Larry saying, "Whatever you do, don't trip when you're holding this box of cards." I didn't trip and I very carefully fed the stacks of cards into the maw of this technological monstrosity. Like the modern miracle it was, the giant computer spit out exactly the information Larry needed for his thesis.

The title of his thesis (which I still have a copy of) was "A Conservative Coalition in The United States Senate." The point of the thesis was to identify a conservative senatorial interparty coalition. To quote the document… "Rather than define a conservative coalition on geographic, party, or other grounds, I hope to identify such a bipartisan grouping through cluster bloc analysis. I also will try to identify its issues of cohesiveness by quantitatively studying its members' roll call responses in the sessions of 1959 and 1963." Obviously, the monstrous IBM computer was key to his research.

The day before his thesis was due, Larry spent the entire night in our cramped apartment typing his narrative. I had given him a portable typewriter for our wedding and on that portable typewriter he did his entire thesis. Early the next morning he dashed out just in time to get it to the bookbinders. Both of us breathed a sigh of relief when he got a wonderful grade.

Those special moments of working together as a team were something I cherished. Larry and I not only loved each other, we liked each other and easily fell into a comfortable routine of doing things together. It was what had been missing in the early years of my parents' marriage and it was what I always knew I wanted in mine.

In September 1967, Larry graduated from Princeton with high marks and started his post-graduate, three-year program at Yale Law School. We moved to New Haven where I got the world's best job at the Yale New Haven Hospital. Ironically, the nurse I replaced at the Medical Group in Princeton due to her move to New Haven was the same nurse I replaced at Yale New Haven, this time due to the pending birth of her second child! I was part of a very prestigious cancer research team and wore a white coat rather than a nurse's uniform. My job consisted of running a Tuesday 'Head and Neck' clinic and a Thursday Leukemia/Lymphoma clinic. The remaining days of the week, I was on call for various patient tests and treatments. We were living on my paycheck, which kept us afloat and enabled Larry to devote himself entirely to his studies and to being captain of the Yale Rugby Club. We were living in a bubble of connubial bliss, completely unaware of the cataclysmic events that 1968 would bring.

EVER SINCE THE 1950S, America had been in a long running war with communist North Vietnam. In January of 1968, North Vietnam launched a major offensive in which thousands of American soldiers stationed in South Vietnam, were killed. With over 500,000 troops already committed to a highly unpopular war, a call went out for an additional 250,000 men sparking a massive outrage in the already vocal anti-war movement. Violent protests against the Vietnam War flooded the nightly news. To avoid the draft, some young men sought refuge in college or parental deferments; others intentionally failed aptitude tests; thousands fled to Canada while the politically connected sought refuge in the National Guard. The Selective Service's deferment system meant that men of lower socioeconomic standing were most likely to be sent to the front lines. In an effort aimed toward fairness, the draft was replaced by a lottery system in which all young men born between 1944 and 1951 were required to report for duty, according to their birthdate.

Larry was now a year and a half into his studies at Yale. At first, we thought he would be excluded from the draft because of his student deferment status. Then, we started hearing rumors that every young man was eligible to go to Vietnam, even the guys who were married and those who were in graduate school. Our concerns became real when the assigned number for Larry's birthdate, #148, came up in the lottery. All men born on April 16th, were to report for duty. Within hours, the Army got ahold of him to let him know that he would be recruited into the Infantry. This was serious. Larry was not opposed to serving his country, but he didn't want to do it as a "grunt."

Because he was a Yale law student, we were able to talk with the Air Force, the Navy, the Army, and the Marine Corps to ask if they could accept him in an officer program. He got accepted into all of them. He took the offer from the Naval Academy because it was just up the road from New Haven to Rhode Island and we could still be geographically connected. We figured he'd probably never be deployed overseas or if he was, he would be safer on a ship somewhere, shooting at the enemy rather than being shot at on the ground or in the air.

In January 1969, I dropped him off at the Naval Academy to start Offi-
cers' Training. On weekends, I'd drive up in my Volkswagen bug, stop in
Mystic, Connecticut, where my dearest childhood friends, Irene and Jack
McCarthy lived. I would spend an amazing overnight with them fawning
over me like I was an honored guest; then I'd drive up to Newport, Rhode
Island and hang out with Larry.

The training took about three and a half months and it was at least a
few weeks into the training before wives were even allowed to visit their
husbands. During the entire time, the men were under all kinds of crazy
restrictions: no touching, no kissing, no hugging. As if that wasn't bad
enough, there was the shock of seeing Larry with all his beautiful wavy
blonde hair, shaved clean. And all the saluting! Everywhere we walked he'd
be doing all this saluting. After being in the super liberal atmosphere of
Princeton and Yale, that was a jolt. I could see Larry's whole demeanor and
personality undergo a change.

Even though Larry was now in the military, my sympathies toward the
anti-war movement never changed. That resulted in a lot of trouble with
my father, a dyed-in-the-wool Marine, who didn't want to hear any criticism about the war and U.S. foreign policy in Southeast Asia. He and I had
some go-arounds that were historic. In the meantime, Larry had to decide
what he wanted to do in the Navy. We had talked about the possibility of
getting assigned to a diesel submarine. The submarine school and base were
located in New London, Connecticut, and it wouldn't disrupt our lives too
much because I would be able to join Larry. Plus, diesels, unlike the nuclear
subs, are short range and not likely to be sent very far from home. So that
was the assignment he put down as his first choice.

My friends, the McCarthys, knew people at the Naval Academy and
through them we were invited to have dinner on a submarine. The officers'
table was the size of an ice cream parlor booth, but we managed to snuggle
in, have a lovely dinner, and go on a tour of the ship afterwards. Larry
came out of that tour knowing there was no way he could spend so much
time under water in that kind of vessel. The following Monday he went to
his officer and said, "Sir, I spent the evening on a submarine, and I don't

think it's a good match for me. I would like you to consider some other deployment." Quite possibly, something had gone wrong with this officer that day or maybe he generally had it in for "Ivy League types," because he completely flipped out, took it as a personal offense, and started swearing and tossing paperwork around.

As a result, the month before graduation, when everyone else got their placement, Larry didn't get his. Even at graduation, we didn't know where he was being assigned. It was a not-so-subtle form of punishment. I, being my liberal Princetonian self, mouthed off about the way we were being treated and apparently it was overheard. I got written up and the Navy brass officially informed Larry that I looked like a "problem wife" and they were keeping an eye on me. I zipped it right up. I never wanted to be the cause of any trouble with the Navy, for Larry or me. That was a real eye opener about what it meant to be a military wife.

One day while we were anxiously waiting for Larry's assignment to come up, he blurted out, "Have you ever heard of the Seabees?" I had seen a John Wayne movie, "The Fighting Seabees," about a Naval unit that not only fought in combat, but also constructed airfields and bases in the most dangerous war zones. "Yeah. What about them?"

"I've been assigned to the Seabees," Larry said. "I'm shipping out to Da Nang." My heart dropped. Da Nang was one of the most dangerous posts in all of Vietnam just ten miles south of the South Vietnam/North Vietnam border with an exceedingly high death rate of American personnel.

I knew for sure, that even though Larry may have been a star of his class at the Naval Academy, graduating in the top fifty, that officer had it in for him and had decided, Larry "was going deep." Graduate students, college students, and married men were not supposed to get that kind of assignment. In addition, I had just taken a pregnancy test and it had turned out positive. It was a triple whammy. I was bawling my eyes out, wondering, "How could they possibly do this?" And all the while still dealing with a father who didn't want to believe this stuff goes on in the military.

Finally, we got a lucky break. Shortly before Larry shipped out, we learned that in the Seabees, like all other Naval divisions, there was a need for the JAGs, the legal arm of the military, which Larry qualified for because he had some legal experience. Thankfully, he was accepted into the program. That got us a reprieve for another three months while he took a special training course in Newport, Rhode Island. I left my job in New Haven and moved up to be with him for those final weeks. We stayed in this crazy mansion that had been broken up into apartments, giving us the strangest bedroom, living room, kitchen arrangement I've ever encountered.

Once my pregnancy was confirmed, I was alternately thrilled at the idea of motherhood and how it would keep me busy while Larry was away, and frightened by the prospect of giving birth with my husband overseas – exactly as my mother had done. But in my tenth week I began to bleed -- right in the middle of a dinner party we were giving at our place for another Navy couple. They were, of course, concerned and sweetly volunteered to stay and await the outcome. Being an officer's wife, I was immediately seen by a Navy doctor who examined me and then shocked me with a false pregnancy diagnosis. His conclusion was I was just experiencing a false pregnancy and that this was not uncommon with wives of deploying husbands. Something about his diagnosis didn't seem right. I was a nurse. I knew my body. I recognized the physical changes -- swollen breasts, extreme fatigue, aversion to bacon -- that didn't come from a normal menstrual cycle. We returned to our party with the news, only somewhat embarrassed by the implications of a "there, there little wifey" diagnosis.

A day or so later, Larry finished his legal program and was ordered to report to Gulfport, Mississippi, where the Battalion 62 Seabees were based. We had already planned to head down to Princeton to see my family before his deployment. The long drive was uneventful and we were welcomed with open arms by Margo and Dod, despite their sadness over the lost pregnancy. It wasn't a day or two later when the severe cramping and bleeding began. I'll never forget the bathroom scene; me stark naked hemorrhaging into the toilet with Mom and Dad holding my hand. I was soon whisked away to the same medical group doctors I has previously worked for. One of the OB/GYNs got only as far as an interview when he said, "Of course there was a pregnancy." This was then confirmed upon examination. I had had a miscarriage. The doctor immediately took me in to surgery and performed a D&C. That know-nothing Navy doctor had risked my life with his misdiagnosis. But I had no recourse. Navy wives didn't lodge complaints against Naval personnel, and I certainly didn't want to stir up any more problems that might reflect badly on Larry or me.

We had to be in Mississippi by a certain date, so the next day we hopped in the car and headed for Gulfport, Mississippi where Larry would spend a month being trained for his Vietnam duty. All during the ride down, Larry was very kind and concerned about my condition. He kept checking on me to make sure I was okay. He could see that the D&C had left me in shaky condition. I knew that once my hormones settled down, I would be back to my usual self. We were on to our next adventure and I didn't wallow in my sorrow for very long.

We stopped in Jacksonville, Florida, to see Larry's parents for what I imagined would be an emotional goodbye before we headed west. Larry's father, Stan, was a WWII B-24 bombardier who had flown twenty-five missions over Germany. He knew first-hand the horrors of war. Larry's mother had lived through the nightmare that only war wives know. I could only imagine their feelings about sending their son off to Vietnam. I thought this was going to be very difficult for them. Much to my surprise, their response was perfunctory. It was all small talk and general niceties, as if Larry was going off to a new job. All I could imagine was that they didn't want their emotions to be a burden to Larry. They were part of the "greatest generation" and had already been through the Depression, WWII, and the Korean War. They were so stoic that they held in all their feelings. You never heard a word of complaint about the scary part of the war and I realized it was just the same as my father never talking about the terrors of Bougainville.

We arrived in Mississippi on July 4th weekend, bloody hot, and humid. Mississippi in July? Uh, uh. You don't want to be there. And we had no place to stay. The Navy hadn't arranged for any accommodations, and it was up to us to find somewhere to live.

We drove along the coast of Mississippi, craning our necks looking for anything resembling a vacancy sign. In the meantime, torrential rainstorms were blowing in off the coast. At one point, I got out of the car and ran up to the office of this U-shaped brick condo in the coastal town of Pass Christian. I was completely drenched. I must have looked like a drowned rat, because the guy in the office took real pity on me. He called up somebody who owned one of the condos and said, "They're willing to rent it to you for as long as you need it." Being military in a military town surely helped. So now we had a place to stay, but without a stick of furniture in it. We had sleeping bags – it was camping out. But at least it was safe and a real place. We rented a TV and sat on the floor to watch astronaut Neil Armstrong take that "one small step" off the Eagle landing module and onto the moon on July 20, 1969.

A lot of other Navy people were staying in the same building and we all became friends. They were of lower rank than Larry, but it didn't matter, they were fun and we all went out crabbing together. There was a quarter-mile pier across the highway and we could go out there and get fresh-caught flounder for breakfast in the morning. That was a real treat.

Larry completed his training and just before he was set to deploy, our lives were upended once again. A major hurricane was brewing off Gulfport and we were evacuated. Three days later, Hurricane Camille, the second most intense tropical cyclone to ever strike the United States, decimated the entire Gulfport Region flattening nearly everything along the coast of Mississippi and killing more than 259 people. We got out just in time.

Larry and I headed back to Princeton and a couple of days later my parents and I drove him to LaGuardia Airport, where he boarded a commercial airline to take him to Vietnam. I tried to put on a brave face as I kissed him goodbye. But on the way home I was in the backseat sobbing away and my parents said, "No crying! You've got to be strong." They were World War II people, they didn't understand this was a different and very unpopular war.

CHAPTER 6

Vietnam and Back

1969-1971

The rotation schedule for the Seabees was very different from everyone else's. The men would be "in country" for six months and then sent home for a month or two and then go back for another six months. You'd have these rotations until your four years were up. Larry and I wrote to each other every day. That was our chief method of communication. We also made audio tapes which we sent to each other. Another way for us to communicate was via short wave radio. There were radio "hams" all over the world who would relay phone calls to the soldiers from people at home. Our intermediary ham was in Hawaii. He would listen in and when one of us signaled the end of our statement by announcing "Over," the ham operator would switch over to the other caller. These guys listened in to everything we said. That was the best technology at the time and it was the only way you could actually talk to your loved ones.

There were stories that we didn't dare mention on the short-wave calls but that we did talk about in our letters. Stories of how ridiculous the whole war was, how Americans were bombing Americans because they got the math wrong and how, as Larry described it, he and his men had to seek shelter underground in what they call "hootches" to avoid being hit by their own troops. As for me, I was scared all the time and barely getting through the day; constantly fighting with my father over stupid things.

By the middle of 1969, the anti-war movement had a tangible effect. President Richard Nixon had been informed by Congress they were cutting off all his funding for the war. Suddenly, it felt like something big was going to happen. Possibly the war was going to end or maybe there would be a major drawdown of troops. We didn't know what it was, but we knew a change was coming.

I started thinking about our future. I couldn't stay with my parents much longer. It was getting too uncomfortable. I decided to drive to Mississippi and set up a home for when Larry came back. I had this great Mustang, I love road trips, so the next time we talked I let Larry know my plan. He said, "Listen, hang in there; there's a list coming out of officers who will be eligible for discharge and maybe my name will be on it."

A few days later a phone call came through in the middle of the night. My mother answered it and shook me awake, "I think it's Larry calling." I stumbled to the phone breathlessly. It was the Hawaiian guy, he had Larry on the short-wave radio. He connected Larry who gushed out, "Don't move, my name is on the list. I'm coming home. I'll see you in Princeton." My heart was so full of gratitude, that for once, I was practically speechless. I turned to my mother, who was anxiously standing by, and said "Larry's going to be back early; he's getting out." Her reply? "Thank God you didn't have that baby."

Her words cut me to the core. I know she didn't purposely mean to hurt me, and I rationalized that she meant that because Larry would return to law school I would have to return to working full time and that would have been very difficult with a baby. At least I hoped that was what she meant. The next morning, I asked my father if he had overheard Mom and me during the night. He hadn't so I relayed the exciting news about the drawdown of troops and Larry's return home. He put down his newspaper, paused a bit and then shared his thought, "What a waste of time and taxpayer's money spent on all that training and uniforms." Not a single word of gratitude that Larry, the son-in-law they both loved so dearly, was being returned to us, safely. I would have thought they would be joyful to have their son-in-law out of harm's way, but they didn't say a word. It was mind boggling to me. Sadly, their self-centered reactions were not what I needed at that moment, and it struck me how blatantly we reveal our true selves in unexpected situations.

Larry gave me the date of his return which would give us just enough time to connect with a few friends and family and attend the November 14th football game against Yale – how perfect – before heading for a quick stop in Jacksonville to visit his family and then on to Mississippi where he would complete the necessary time and paperwork for leaving the military.

On November 13th, several days before Larry's scheduled return, in the middle of the afternoon there was a knock on the door, I opened it and unexpectedly, there he stood, a looming military presence, filling the doorway, just like my father had done all those many years ago. I later learned that Larry had decided to surprise me by arriving days earlier and that 'all' of Princeton was in on the plan. I leapt into his arms, wrapped my legs around him and hugged and kissed him with all my might, vowing that nothing would ever tear us apart again.

EARLIER IN THE MONTH, my mother and I had shopped for the perfect negligée – long and sexy with side slits right up to my waist. My parents had booked that night for us at the Princeton Inn and Larry and I wasted no time heading straight there. The next morning, we were off to Palmer stadium for the football game where we only stayed until half time. We were eager to head out for Jacksonville, Florida and our final destination, Gulfport, Mississippi. We left the stadium, climbed into the car, which was already packed, and headed South.

WHEN WE ARRIVED IN GULFPORT, there was nothing left of the town we had known. Hurricane Camille had flattened most of the buildings. We couldn't even find our way around because all of our usual landmarks were gone, whether it be street signs, restaurants, public buildings, or churches. Boats, including a tugboat, were lying helter skelter blocks inland. Entire neighborhoods were gone. With great difficulty, we were able to get our bearings and find the lot where our beachside condo once stood. We couldn't believe our eyes — all that was left was a U-shaped concrete slab, a mud-filled swimming pool and a forsaken diving board.

Processing out of the Navy would take from six to eight weeks and in the meantime, the military put us up in one of the emergency trailers they used to accommodate homeless navy personnel. As luck would have it, our trailer was parked right next to Larry's boss, Captain John Paul Jones, and his wife, Winkie. Captain Jones was Larry's In Country Superior Commander. Winkie would start on the vodka martinis around four o'clock in the afternoon and her husband would come home and quickly catch up with her. Almost every night, he would demand we come to dinner at their place, where we'd spend the night being lectured about how the Navy really needed educated, smart guys like Larry. Larry told me later the Captain had expressed that same sentiment during what the Navy calls a Hail & Farewell party before leaving Vietnam. These ceremonies were given at the end or beginning of an officer's tour of duty. Because Larry was released two and a half years early, he had the great distinction of being hailed and farewelled at the same time having spent a total of ninety-three days at war. The Captain told me straight to my face I was the reason why Larry wasn't staying in the Navy and he was really disappointed that a guy like Larry could be "pussy-whipped" by someone like me. I kept my mouth shut. I had learned my lesson; when you're in the service, you don't say a thing. I could hardly wait until the required time and paperwork would be completed and we'd have Gulfport at our backs.

As if things weren't bad enough, we were T-boned by an uninsured driver at a fairly high speed in our beautiful Mustang. The car was totaled, and I was pretty banged up. It was painful for me to stand or sit due to my knee ending up in the glove compartment and my coccyx sandwiched in my seat by a backseat passenger who wasn't wearing his seatbelt.

Larry was struggling to finish all his discharge paperwork and we fell into this terrible routine of me in pain and him itching to get all this over with. After the first excitement of his return, Larry wasn't himself. He became severely depressed, sometimes breaking down and crying for seemingly no reason. He was unrecognizable and just dragged himself through the day. He wouldn't touch me, hug me, come near me. I didn't know what to say or do to help him.

During his time in Vietnam, Larry was stationed in Dong Ha, the northernmost town in South Vietnam. His unofficial title was Shitty Little Jobs Officer. One of those shitty jobs entailed writing to the families of the guys who had been killed, informing them of the death of their loved one. It must have been horrific for him. He flatly refused to discuss even one case. To add insult to injury, deploying and returning military personnel were transported using civilian aircraft which ended up being a surreal experience for them. I remember Larry telling me how shocking it was to be in-country one minute and then be seated next to a fellow American on a commercial plane who had no idea what Larry had been through.

I was desperate to get my husband back, to find a way to snap him out of it. Then I remembered that at some point in my life, I had read that when Greek warriors came back from battle, in order to take the war out of them, there were women who were assigned to bed them. Apparently in their culture, this was a normal practice. You would take the war out of men by making sure they made love. So instead of giving Larry his space and allowing him to wallow in his misery, I coerced, urged and seduced him to have sex with me. He finally gave in and the next day he was a different man. Larry and I never discussed it. All I know is whatever happened, it lifted some dark cloud and the next day he was the old Larry I had seen off to war ninety-three days earlier.

In that one year between January and December 1969, we'd experienced Officers' Candidacy School, Navy Law training, a miscarriage, separation, Vietnam, a car accident, and severe depression. We were only too happy to get back to New Haven so Larry could finish his final eighteen months of Yale Law School and we could get on with our lives.

ONCE WE WERE HOME, Larry settled in quickly, both with his studies and his rugby team. I, on the other hand, came back without a job in the cancer research department of Yale New Haven Hospital. My replacement saw no reason to give it back. When I left, I most likely left for good. That job did afford me lots of contacts and potential opportunities so I commandeered an empty office with a desk and a phone. Using the hospital directory, I got my dialing finger busy. It took a week or two, but I did finally get wind of the hospital wanting to start up an IV Team. Two of the three positions were filled already so I rushed myself down to the pharmacy for an interview. When I was running the cancer clinics, I had to learn to insert IVs and to draw blood. In fact, I was the only RN on campus that was certified in these techniques. At the time, IVs were the sole purview of medical students trained with a hit or miss method. Mostly they were unsupervised, much to the chagrin of the unsuspecting patients. An hour later, I came out of the interview as the third and final member of the first IV team ever at Yale. Eight to four, five days a week and no weekends! Another bang-up job for the resume; I was entrusted with creating the team from the ground up.

Upon returning to his second year of law school, Larry and I were able to qualify for student housing. Once we settled in, my 'I want a baby hormones' started surging. I wanted to put the miscarriage behind me and it wasn't long before I started campaigning for a second try. Reluctantly, Larry caved under the pressure and almost exactly to the day of nine months prior to his graduating law school, I did a pregnancy test at the hospital and within a couple of hours we got the news that I was pregnant. This time I sailed easily through the dreaded tenth week and continued to work all through my pregnancy.

Prior to graduation, Larry was already being wined and dined by all the top law firms. He had his pick of where to go. They all wanted him. Then out of the blue, he said, "I really don't want to be a lawyer. I don't want to do that seven-year thing where you have to grind away and hope to become a partner. That's not me. That doesn't appeal to me." Knowing Larry, I figured he already had something in mind. I said, "Fine. What do you want to do?"

There was this one young, burgeoning outfit, Bradford National, a stock transfer company run by a bunch of energetic first-generation Irish guys from New Jersey. They had come scouting for talent at Yale because the law school had a reputation of not just teaching case studies, but of teaching their graduates how to think. These rough-around-the-edges Irish guys decided it was a good idea to see if they could snag one of those smart guys from Yale to help turn their struggling company around. And they did. They got a good one. It was just the kind of challenge Larry loved. The Bradford guys took him out to dinner, offered him a job and on the spot, he accepted. That decision would mark a major turning point in our lives. He didn't discuss his decision with me beforehand. He just went ahead and did it, relying on his instincts that this was just the opportunity he was looking for.

CHAPTER 7

Is This What Adulthood Looks Like?

1971-1973

Right in the middle of Larry's final exams, on June 8, 1971, I gave birth to our daughter Maida – twelve days before my due date. Larry and I were in our apartment enjoying our regular Sunday morning habit of coffee and poppy seed rolls while reading the papers, when lo and behold Maida started to make her presence known with lots of somersaults. A quick call to my obstetrician confirmed it was time, "Come on in, let's get this baby to you." So, we did, and it was in my own hospital so I felt very confident and well taken care of. Many hours later, after I was given an epidural to relieve my pain, Larry was sent home only to return instantly because the baby started to crown. She was delivered in front of an audience of nursing students and medical students and I introduced her to everybody announcing to the world that this was Maida. At that moment, I remember looking at Larry and seeing tears streaming down his cheeks. My immediate thought was, "How embarrassing. I hope no one else sees that." In my mind, I equated tears with weakness; yet I knew that wasn't the case. I knew he was crying with joy. It was that Dodwell military training that said, "Don't show emotion!" That still had a powerful grip on me. I hoped Larry had not sensed my reaction. It was a moment I wished I could take back.

Once I was out of the delivery room, Larry let me know how surprised he was at my announcement of the baby's name. We had discussed names, but I had somehow missed that we hadn't really decided together. Larry wasn't opposed to the name Maida, but it didn't help that when he called his mother to let her know she was a grandmother, her reaction to the baby's name was, "No comment."

On my part, I was feeling total elation. My baby girl was healthy, with all her fingers and toes and I, due to the epidural, had sailed through the delivery with no pain. Maida was absolutely the most gorgeous "blond head," as my father described her and was used as the model for a 'how to bathe your baby' demonstration for all of the new mothers in the maternity ward.

Because of the proximity of all my friends and colleagues in the hospital, I was inundated with more visitors than I probably should have had. A few hours after I gave birth, the spinal shot wore off and I found myself ravaged by the most incredible pain imaginable which reached an unbearable threshold on my first trip to the bathroom. The glut of well-wishers combined with my extreme discomfort eventually took its toll and the doctor had to require a sign on the door stating there were to be no more visitors until further notice – except for the husband.

In Princeton, New Jersey, my parents were anxiously awaiting the moment when they would be told to get in the car and drive up to New Haven to meet their grandchild. Because Larry was in the middle of Yale Law School finals, we knew the last thing he needed was to be in charge of caring for a new mother and infant. We had prearranged that Mom would come in to help me out. But when my complete exhaustion took over, it was decided that Mom and Dad should wait a couple of days to let us catch our breath and let me get a bit of rest. This news was not taken well and my dad felt compelled to call me secretly and say, "You have no idea how this has upset your mother. She can't believe she's going back to work today when they all expected her to be dashing off to New Haven to be there for you and the baby." This was the last thing I needed to hear. I was in no mood to be lectured at by my dad. I let him have his say and then told him that as far as I was concerned, Larry was doing the right thing by taking charge of the schedule because it was what the doctors had advised. I had to tell him,

"Dad, please don't make me choose between you and my husband. Just so you know, it will be Larry."

A day or two later, without the benefit of car seats or seat belts, we managed to make the drive from the hospital to our apartment. I was holding Maida in my arms, stiff legged in fear of any situation where we'd have to brake. It was a nerve wracking and scary ride. To my amazement, I came home to discover that Larry had made a major change. He remembered the pediatrician saying, "I don't recommend having your baby sleep in the same room with you. I think you should always have a separate room for the baby." Larry took that seriously and without my knowing, he turned his office into a nursery. I thought that was just fine!

It was June and it was bloody hot in Connecticut, especially in our unair conditioned, second story, garden apartment. On our first day home from the hospital, Larry decided it was his duty to provide us with a real home-cooked meal. He went grocery shopping and bought pork chops and God knows what else – I remember strawberry ice cream, which was never one of my favorites – but I could hear him toiling downstairs in this tiny kitchen trying to come up with the best dinner possible for the two of us. Maida was sleeping quietly in her crib in her new little room just off the bedroom and Larry came up with two trays of food. I was sitting propped up in bed and Larry was sitting in a bedroom chair and we're just ready to settle down with our meals on our laps when who starts to cry, but Maida. The two of us looked at each other for a brief moment before both spontaneously bursting into tears. We realized at the same nano-second that life was never going to be the same.

A day or so later my mother, who by now had calmed down, was dropped off by my dad. He turned around and went straight back to Princeton. With her role as "Mother's Helper" re-established, we shared two of the best weeks ever as mother and daughter. After having been hurt, she really rose to the occasion. In her mind, she had been thwarted and rejected while to me, she didn't understand what I was going through. Nevertheless, she was there for bringing the baby to me when Maida needed nursing and helping with meals. For those two weeks, she couldn't have been more perfect. Both she and Larry were right there any time of the day or night. They'd hear Maida cry and bring her right to me. Then one day, I made the mistake of saying, "You know what? I'm feeling pretty good, I can get up and around; I kind of feel more like myself." That was it. Never saw them again. And to add insult to injury, both Larry and my mother completely tuned out Maida's crying. They would say, "Oh, did she get up in the middle of the night?" I took over the role of always being the one on call. I wasn't upset. I just thought it was an interesting and unexpected phenomenon.

The other advantage of having my mom there was that it enabled Larry to get through his exams. Before she left, we presented her with a charm for her bracelet, which was two tiny booties, one with Maida's name on it and the other with her birth date, to commemorate that she had held us together during that crucial time.

∽

NATURALLY, LARRY SAILED THROUGH his exams and was chomping at the bit to start his new job at Bradford National's headquarters in Manhattan. Maida was only two-weeks old when it was time for us to move. He had rented a small house in Westport, Connecticut, an easy train ride from Manhattan, and he and a friend spent the whole night packing a truck with all our belongings. In the morning, off they drove to Westport, followed by me in our car with my mother holding Maida on her lap, to settle into our very first house.

Westport was on the Long Island Sound at the mouth of the Saugatuck River, a charming early Colonial township steeped in history dating back to the American Revolution. It was a bedroom community filled with artists, musicians, authors, and upwardly mobile families. Most of the inhabitants had relocated from the city to the suburbs enticed by the ease of commuting to their offices in New York in the morning and returning in the evening to the rolling hills and gentle seaside beauty of Westport.

Our rented house was a two-story wooden structure with rooms hardly bigger than the garden apartment we had left in New Haven. I don't think it was more than 1,200 square feet. It had what they called three bedrooms, but two of them were tiny and the master bedroom was probably not much more than 10' x 15'. Still, it was definitely a step up from that starter apartment in Princeton. We had a house. We had a baby. We felt like grownups.

We moved in with the bare necessities, a bed, a crib, and the requisite rocking chair for nursing a newborn. Making the move with an infant was daunting. But I was sure that with my mother's help I could manage. Unfortunately, the day we arrived, my mother informed me that Dod was anxious for her to come home and he would be picking her up that afternoon. As soon as she left, I felt panicky. How would I ever cope by myself? Larry was starting his job in Manhattan and would be gone most of the day.

At the time, we had only one car, another Mustang (my grandmother loaned us the money), which replaced the one we lost in the accident. At first, I tried driving Larry to the train station in the morning and picking him up at night. But with Maida still an infant, it became impossible. His return time was never certain, and I would find myself sitting in the parking lot of the train station at nine or ten o'clock at night trying to nurse a squalling infant in the backseat of the Mustang — not an easy thing to do. Finally, we decided that it would be best if he took the car in the morning, left it at the station and drove himself home at night.

I had been eagerly looking forward to motherhood and family life, but not in the way it was playing out. Our first summer together as a married couple consisted of moving to Westport, where I knew nobody, had no friends, without a car, and with a two-week-old baby. Instead of my fantasy of suburban bliss, I found myself at the beck and call of a nursing infant and endlessly awaiting a husband who was immersed in a new and exciting adventure that didn't include me. It was a shock to my whole system. We went from being partners in crime to me feeling as if the rug had been pulled out from under me. All the things that made me feel relevant were gone: my nursing career, my personal freedom, and the enjoyment that Larry and I shared working as a team.

Larry's job at Bradford National was all-consuming. That summer, as part of their major reshuffling, the company made the decision to change from paper transfers to computers. They would spend endless nights and weekends making the switch. The changeover took all of the summer and then some. Larry would leave at six o'clock in the morning and wouldn't come home until way past dinner, sometimes even as late as ten or eleven o'clock at night. Often, he was too exhausted to do anything but fall into bed. My one source of joy was Maida. She was a delight — smart, sweet, and beautiful. Larry and I had both looked forward to having a baby. He had helped raise a couple of younger brothers and was comfortable around children. When he was home, he was very attentive to Maida, but the problem was that he was hardly ever home.

Once I got over the resentment of having to give up my previous life, I settled into motherhood and enjoyed Maida tremendously; still, the company of an infant is not the same as the company of an adult partner. I was eager for adult stimulation.

The street we lived on, Wild Rose Road, was a dead-end and our driveway was a convenient turn-around. Whenever I would hear the crunching of gravel, I'd go running out the front door hoping it was somebody I could talk too. Most of the time it wasn't.

On the weekends when Larry was home, he played rugby. That worked out well for him. I certainly could understand how after a grueling week at Bradford he needed some physical activity. I would follow after him carrying Maida in my arms and do the "rugby wife" thing. But again, it was all about him. I had become merely a useful appendage. None of my emotional needs were being met. Slowly, I started becoming resentful and hurt and most of all, lonely.

Like most women of my generation, it was ingrained in me that my job in life was to acquiesce to my husband's wishes and in return I would enjoy a happy and compatible marriage. But in this new arrangement, acquiescing meant giving up all my wants and needs for very little in return. I soon discovered I was not the only woman who felt that way.

It was the beginning of the Women's Movement and Gloria Steinem was running around saying "Wake up! You have needs too and you should have expectations and you shouldn't be the one that feels bad because you're requesting something." The big take-way from the Women's Movement was the idea that motherhood is okay, but careers are better – or equally important.

So, there I was, this odd twenty-six-and-a-half year old who was still part of the 1950s/1960s mentality, while a majority of girls my age were already thinking, "Hell, I don't need to get married now; I'm having a career." I was eager to be part of this new conversation, but it felt as if I had excluded myself because I was already married and had a baby. It was a confusing time. I was being pulled in a lot of different directions and I didn't have a close circle of friends to help me explore my feelings and come up with solutions to my unexpressed frustrations.

The main activity of my day was pushing Maida in her carriage to the nearby shopping area and hoping that along the way I might run in to one the famous Westport residents like Paul Newman or Robert Redford or Jason Robards. That would be a highlight of my day – some exciting bit of news I could share with Larry – if he was interested. I was becoming aware of how desperate I was for any morsel of adult conversation and how bored I was with myself. I always needed some new project or adventure in my life and I soon found one.

Larry and I had been renting the Dutch Colonial house on Wild Rose Road for almost a year when we decided to buy it. From the day we first moved in, I had seen the possibility that with an interior reconstruction, the house could be made a lot more livable. There was a cramped living room and a small dining room that didn't get much use. To me it was a waste of space. I knew that if I could get rid of the dining room, more light would come in from the windows and we would have a much bigger living room. Larry was doing well at Bradford and he was okay with the cost of the renovation – probably because it kept me busy with a creative project and took my mind off of how absent he was.

The day after escrow closed, I had the dining room archway taken out. As soon as the archway removal was completed, I redecorated the entire living room. I was dazzled by a quilted fabric couch that was lime and celery green and white. Floral. Very pretty. Naturally, I had to have matching wall-to-wall carpet, which was celery wool. It turned out beautifully even though I made some minor mistakes. Having a one-year old meant that both the couch and rug were impossible to keep clean. This was my first attempt at fixing up a house and I was learning what to do and what not to do, the hard way.

I had no way of knowing it then, but the pleasure of remodeling and upgrading old houses and eventually building new ones would become a major part of my life and a satisfying use of my artistic talents.

AROUND THE TIME MAIDA turned two, I discovered that the nearby high school offered adult evening classes. One of the subjects was art. I thought the least I could do was go out once a week and hang out with grown-ups. I found a reliable babysitter and signed up for an adult art class at the local high school. That class turned out to be a godsend.

Most of the people in the class were retirees who, like me, painted for pleasure. I knew nothing about the art world. Through them I found out there were local art shows, which were presented at parks and high school gyms. The teacher encouraged me to show my work, so I put together a collection of paintings I had done and along with some of the other students I began to exhibit my work. Much to my surprise, I was winning blue ribbons. Finally, I had something to look forward to on weekends during the spring and summer.

CHAPTER 8

Trapped in the "Burbs"

1974-1978

I was completely ignorant about what was going on in Larry's work life. When he came home, the last thing either of us wanted to talk about was his work. All I knew was that he was doing well enough to buy a house and fix it up. Larry gave me a regular allowance to run the household and expected me to stay within a strict budget. As long as I did, he had no complaints. Having grown up with a mother who was extremely frugal, I was very conscientious about spending money-maybe even obsessive. I devoted a lot of time figuring out how to renovate the kitchen to make it more functional, but I never did anything about it because I wasn't sure we could actually afford to do the renovation. Larry didn't share anything about our finances with me, so I had no real sense about where we stood and what we could or could not afford.

After about two years in Westport, Larry and I got hungry for a nicer, more grown-up house. I found this great salt box shaped colonial on Reichert Circle that was painted barn red with black trim. It was a lot bigger than where we were living and we bought it. There had been a good-sized extension made to one corner of the house: a room with a vaulted ceiling, a walk-in closet, and a nice bathroom. The wall that held both the closet door and the bathroom door was shaped like the side of a barn. That image inspired my next renovation.

I hired a contractor and had him add real old barn beams to the vaulted ceiling to give it some architectural interest. He found some wonderful weather-beaten boards which I had him put up on the wall giving it even more of a barn look. I was just thrilled with the whole thing and said something to the contractor like, "Wow, this looks great." He said, "Yep, and when the next person comes along and buys this house the first thing they're gonna' do is take down that wall." That stopped me for a minute. Then I realized the truth of his words – just as I had disrupted the prior owner's vision, I had to assume that it would happen to me, too. The next person might take down those beautiful, weathered boards.

From that minute on, I accepted the fact that everything in life is temporary. I would enjoy my handiwork while I could, but I wasn't going to be emotionally attached to any one place. I'd fix it up, redo it the way I liked and move on.

⌒⌒○

WHEN MAIDA ENTERED KINDERGARTEN, I made my first close friend in Westport. Her name was Betsy and her daughter was in the same kindergarten class as Maida. Betsy had four other children, all boys and she was a good ten years older than me, but we shared a similar mind set and enjoyed each other's company. Betsy was my saving grace because where I tended to be anxious and emotional, she was cool, calm, and collected. I needed that kind of stabilizing influence in my life because Larry's career was soaring and the demands on his time and attention were out of control. He had no time to listen to me, to be a shoulder to cry on, and to co-parent Maida. The picture we had painted of our marriage was that of a commuter husband working hard to give us all the luxuries in life that we could wish for and I was to be the dutiful stay-at-home mom beautifying our nest. It was a stereotype that needed torching.

Maida and I could no longer count on Larry to be home for dinner. If I would question our lifestyle or say, "We miss you," he would just shut down. It was obvious that whatever was happening in New York was more important to him than what was happening in Westport. His work had overtaken his life and I was tired of begging him to pay attention to us. I found myself dwelling on my misery and I didn't like who I was becoming.

By the early 1970s, New Age thinking had permeated western culture. We were in mystical, spiritual, transcendental overdrive. One of the most pervasive ideas that came out of that era was a belief that each of us is responsible for our own happiness. That wasn't just New Age gobbledygook. Even Abraham Lincoln famously said, "Most folks are as happy as they make up their mind to be." I decided it was time to make myself happy. If Larry wasn't going to pay attention to me, I would pay attention to myself.

In 1974, I saw an article in the local newspaper about a group of artists who had been instructors at The Famous Artists School in Westport. The school, which offered correspondence classes in art had started in the early 1940s at a time when correspondence classes first came into vogue. These long-distance art classes were often advertised on matchbook covers and in magazines depicting a profile line-drawing of a girl with an upturned nose, accompanied by the slogan, "Draw Me." Several different schools offered the same kind of remote instruction, but the Westport school was one of the most well-known. The illustration staff included big name artists like Norman Rockwell and Stevan Dohanos. Students would send work to them through the mail which would be critiqued by instructors far less famous than Rockwell and Dohanos, but were accomplished artists in their own right and had solid credentials.

The article in the local paper told the story of how after more than twenty years, the company which had once been one of Westport's beloved businesses, had closed down. In a generous act of gratitude, the company had provided the four remaining faculty members with a studio space where they could practice their art. The four artists turned the space into a school, where they were currently accepting new students. The idea of working with these artists appealed to me, especially because the studio was within walking distance of my house.

I made that short walk and found myself in an old thread mill on the Saugatuck River, which looked like my idea of a Parisian salon. It was very Bohemian, big enough to have a makeshift kitchen, beat up couches and chairs, easels and, best of all, very good light. Over the next few years, I would spend a lot of time taking lessons there.

Whenever I could find a babysitter or when Larry would occasionally come home on time, I was at the studio. Those four art teachers became my circle of friends. With them I felt supported, relevant, and respected. I could feel my creative juices flowing again, not only in my art but in other aspects of my life as well. I was experiencing a rekindled sense of self-worth and with it came a confidence that I could try new things.

~

AT THE SAME TIME, I had caught the construction bug. Following the success of the wall removal at Wild Rose Road and the barn board paneling at Reichert Circle, I wanted another house to renovate. I convinced Larry to let me purchase a tiny Cape Cod house I had found close to the Westport beach. I sold him on the idea that this would take my "project management" skills up a notch; not only would I renovate the house, I would rent it out.

There had been some unspoken pressure from Larry about me holding my own a bit in the financial department. He didn't want to come right out and say it, but I think deep down he resented the fact that I was spending money on houses and renovations. He failed to acknowledge that my efforts were increasing the value of our properties. I *was* holding my own – he just didn't recognize it. Then, as a way to stop my complaining and support my idea of contributing to the family income through rental properties, he gave me the okay to buy the Cape Cod house

~

IT WAS A CIRCA 1950-60s bungalow consisting of a living room, kitchen, two bedrooms, a bathroom, and an open loft above the living area. I especially liked the loft because it reminded me of my grandparents Lake Mohawk vacation home, where I spent so many enjoyable summers.

The design/build team was comprised of me and a local contractor. The upgrade was mostly cosmetic, consisting of fresh paint, both interior and exterior, new wall to wall carpeting, new kitchen cabinets, counter tops, sink, fixtures, and appliances, all purchased at the local building supply store. I watched in amazement how confidently the contractor and his team of construction workers demolished the whole kitchen in a matter of hours. The adrenaline surge I experienced during that demolition became a drug of choice which never diminished. No matter how many projects I would eventually tackle, the demolition remained my favorite part of the remodeling process.

The transformation of the tiny old-fashioned kitchen was accomplished in what I thought was the blink of an eye. I remember thinking "Gee, this is exciting, creative and *social!*" Hanging out with the construction workers was great fun. For the most part, they were good-looking, strong young men who appreciated me and my ideas. They supplemented my need for human interaction and male attention. In their eyes, I mattered.

THERE'S A DIFFERENCE BETWEEN wanting a marriage to end and wanting a marriage to change. In my mind, I never considered divorce but I did take some desperate measures to "renovate and remodel" our marriage which may have appeared to Larry as if I wanted to end it. One day, I was so overcome with the knowledge that my feelings had been left completely out of our marital equation that I announced I was leaving and would be spending the night in New York City. I had no idea what I was going to do. I had never booked a hotel room on my own, but I had been taking an art class in Manhattan at the New School and was confident about taking the train there and back. The idea of just spending a day or two on my own, going to museums and art exhibits had been a remote fantasy, but now some inner voice was crying out "Do something brave, Linda. Show the world who you are!" I obviously wanted to shock Larry into the realization of how bad things were between us, so off I went without any real plan.

I took the train into the city where I knew no one and wandered around aimlessly feeling a curious mix of freedom and guilt. I wound my way over to the Metropolitan Museum leisurely enjoying the exhibit until an officious uniformed guard informed me it was closing time. As I joined the crowd exiting the museum, I experienced a recognizable twinge and knew instantly what it meant – I was about to get my period. I urgently needed to get back inside and get to the ladies' room before the white slacks I was wearing bore evidence of my emergency. Behind me the massive doors had already swung shut. I scurried around the back of the building hoping there might be another entrance. There was, but it too was shut tight. Out of desperation, I began banging on the door crying out, "Please, I have an emergency, somebody please help me." Luckily, my plea reached the ears of a sympathetic worker. Once I explained my panic he couldn't get the door open fast enough. When I finished getting myself together and was back out on the street, I found myself feeling utterly defeated. There was no way I could muster enough chutzpah to act on my threat to spend the night away from home. I hadn't even brought so much as an overnight bag and the thought of finding a proper hotel room was overwhelming. I had started the day with such bravado and now here I was alone, facing the darkness in a city so big it didn't even know I was there. All I could think of was to crawl back home.

When I came home Larry just stared at me. I tried to explain what happened. But he wasn't interested and just went to bed. He said nothing. I said nothing. We never discussed it. Neither of us had effective communications skills. Neither of us were willing to address the problems in our marriage.

THINGS WEREN'T GOING smoothly on the renovation either. I was new at this and just learning. Along the way I made some memorable mistakes. My first big one came on the Cape Cod. Much to my shock, the contractor thought it was a good idea to use a circular saw to sand down the exterior paint, which of course left horribly scarred shingles with circular patterns gouged into their surfaces. I saw what he was doing but I never said a word. Lesson learned? "Remember, I am the boss. The boss with the checkbook." Never again did I let a builder intimidate me or let his mistakes go unnoticed.

BETWEEN MY ART CLASSES and my house renovations, I avoided dwelling on the lack of support or respect I was getting from Larry. In fact, the more deeply involved I was with my creative projects, the more distant he became. The truth was, Larry and I were growing apart.

It was around my thirtieth birthday that I finally came to grips with the reality of my marriage. Thirty is a good time to take a hard look at your life. I already knew that on my birthday, December 8th, there would be no celebration, no special dinner, no surprises, nothing to mark that noteworthy milestone. Larry had made it very clear to me that in December he would be involved with all the office Christmas festivities in New York. There was "a very important party" he had to attend on December 8th. Naturally, it took precedence over my birthday.

The classic image of the office Christmas party — a drunken affair where grown men made fools of themselves with pretty, young secretaries — was not lost on me. Whatever suspicions or emotions I might have felt at his pronouncement, I brushed away as inappropriate. "Never mind your feelings, Linda; there's nothing to be discussed." That's how I dealt with it. Just as my mother had done with my father.

Larry's discounting of my birthday was a perfect opportunity for me to feel sorry for myself, but instead, to prove how evolved I was, I decided to give myself a wonderful birthday present. Gloria Steinem was scheduled to speak at a home in Westport on December 8th. Meeting the famous icon of the Women's Liberation Movement would be a great way to celebrate my birthday. There were questions I was dying to ask Gloria, about how to successfully navigate the role of "wife and mother" along with a career. I was certain she would have the answers. In addition, I was looking forward to getting together with a stimulating group of like-minded women and dipping my toes in the roiling waters of Women's Liberation.

I arranged for a babysitter — a cute young girl who Maida was fond of — and on December 8th I had my hair done, my nails done, and was getting dressed for the much-anticipated evening, when the phone rang. It was my cute young babysitter calling to say, "I've got this terrible cold and I can't make it. I wish I could have told you sooner."

That's when it hit me — it was my thirtieth birthday, my husband was off gallivanting in New York, my babysitter just flaked out on me, and the evening of female empowerment I was so looking forward to was going on without me. It was an apt metaphor for my life.

I was close to tears and could have held a pity party for myself, but to my credit, I pulled on my big girl pants, got my act together, found another babysitter, and in-the-nick-of-time headed off to meet Gloria Steinem. Woman Power! I was feeling it!

When I arrived, the house was already filled to capacity. Women of all ages were sipping wine, munching crudités, and chattering away like mad. The air was crackling with excitement. I looked around to see if there was anyone I knew. That's when I spotted her — my cute, young babysitter.

The minute she saw me her jaw dropped. I walked straight up to her and said, "You know if you had come clean, I would have taken you to this event. I would have driven you here." She went into complete panic, stammered some lame excuse, and disappeared for the rest of the evening. All I could think was, "So much for Sisterhood!"

Fortunately, from that point on, the evening improved markedly. I did get a chance to talk with Gloria Steinem and expressed how torn I felt, "I'm not my mother's generation. I know what her life was like, and I'm rejecting that, but I still have a hard time imagining what my daughter's life will be like. I don't know where I fit in." Gloria was truly empathetic. She may not have had any ready answers, but she was a good listener and made me feel as if I'd been heard. Maybe a sympathetic ear was really all I needed. In any event, Gloria Steinem made my thirtieth birthday memorable. As a result, I became an even bigger Steinem fan and remembered reading in *Ms. Magazine* that she felt her generation, which is ten years older than mine, did not have good mothering. I could identify with that. My mother was disappointed, angry, frustrated -- stuck reading *Good Housekeeping* and *Women's Day* magazines to make her feel as if there was some purpose to her life.

I began to accept the reality that women were perceived as second-class citizens and needed to stand up for themselves. I read, studied, and chatted about the whole business of feminism to anyone who would listen. I became a "true believer" confident in my new ideas and felt I could express them convincingly to anyone who might be interested.

One night, Larry invited a new business connection he had met in New York, over for dinner. His name was Muir Atherton. Muir was related to the esteemed naturalist, John Muir, who was known mainly for the preservation of Yosemite National Park. Muir Atherton was very preppy, very old family, and somewhat intimidating. We were sitting in front of our fireplace chatting away about life in general and after a few glasses of wine, I decided to open up about what I had been up to lately. In a very non-threatening way, I laid out the observations and experiences I had been having in the Women's Liberation Movement. When I got down from my bully pulpit, Muir Atherton took a deep breath, looked me square in the eyes and said, "Have you thought about getting some psychiatric help?" Larry sat there in complete silence. The dinner party took a nosedive. That single cruel blow of Muir's chauvinistic sledgehammer completely shut me down and Larry's failure to come to my defense destroyed whatever confidence I had managed to build up. For at least two years, I didn't say another word regarding what I thought about the inequities between men and women.

～

IN 1978, THINGS TOOK a welcomed turn. Larry came home with the news that he had been asked to relocate to the West Coast. Bradford National had a struggling subsidiary in San Francisco and they were contemplating whether to dump it or not. Larry saw it as a new, exciting challenge and convinced the company to give him a shot at saving their failing entity. They agreed and it was a done deal. That was fine with me. As much as I was enjoying my art classes and my renovations, I couldn't help but blame part of our marital problems on the long-distance lifestyle we were leading. I was eager to get out of Westport and all I could think of was that Larry would now be working in the same city we lived in. Maybe he would have more time for Maida and me. Maybe there was a chance that our flagging marriage would survive. Maybe.

～

ONE OF MY TEACHERS at the Westport art school, Annie Toulmin Rothe, had studied at the San Francisco Art Institute and her praise of their graduate program whet my appetite. I told Larry I'd be happy to move to San Francisco if I could go to art school. He didn't respond enthusiastically, but he didn't say no. Three months later, we sold the salt box house, sold the Cape Cod (both at a profit) and left Connecticut for California – a place I hadn't visited since I was three years old.

CHAPTER 9

Hearts to San Francisco

1979-1982

In January 1979, we moved into a newly built home in Mill Valley in Marin County about five miles outside of San Francisco. Some crafty land speculator had carved out this spectacular site from a seemingly unbuildable rocky, weed filled landscape. The house was like nothing we'd ever seen. It was built on a cliff and our bedroom was downstairs, with a sunken bathtub and a gorgeous view of Richardson Bay. It was very California. Access to the city of San Francisco was about ten minutes across the Golden Gate Bridge. I loved it. Especially the first few months. The weather was superb. On the East Coast, winter was still having its way and all my friends were jealous of my spectacular California vista.

Larry started right in with his new position at Bradford and once I got Maida situated in school, I began investigating SFAI (The San Francisco Art Institute). As soon as I walked into the courtyard of that famous school with its towering Diego Rivera fresco, I knew it was the place for me. Apart from the incredible artistic ambience, the real motivation for me was the challenge of getting a four-year degree. My previous nursing program had only offered a three-year RN diploma. I wanted to be able to say I was the first woman in my family to get a college degree. It was not inexpensive, but I wanted it badly. Larry grudgingly agreed and I signed up for what would become the next chapter of my life.

When I entered SFAI, Maida was in second grade. I was able to organize my class schedule so that I could drop her off for school in the morning and be there when it ended in the afternoon. My "part-time" student status meant it would probably take me more than four years to graduate, but that was okay with me.

I loved the Art Institute. It was the opposite of my nursing school experience where things were done by the book. In art school, everything was in flux. Besides the constant challenge of wrestling with new media – oil paints, watercolors, acrylics – I found myself swept up in a counterculture movement that had affected not only San Francisco, but the rest of the world. Revolutionary concepts about race and gender abounded and beliefs about "flower power" and "free love" had virtually upended all moral codes. It was a heady time for a girl with an East Coast Catholic upbringing and forced me to rethink some of my most deeply ingrained beliefs – especially about love and marriage. This was not something I could discuss with Larry. His head was in a button-down high-rise world that was paying no attention to what was going on in the streets.

Fortunately, at SFAI there were a lot of interesting people to schmooze and laugh with. In no time, I had a whole new group of friends. One of them was Dennis Casey, a Vietnam vet who was majoring in photography. He was handsome, he was talented, and he rode a motorcycle – my kind of guy!

Right away, Dennis and I became best buddies. Initially, we shared a strong physical attraction, but the basis of our friendship went far beyond that. We were kindred souls. Before long, Dennis began to confide in me about his troubled past, which included a father who beat him unmercifully and his years in Vietnam as a "tunnel rat," where it was his perilous duty to go into enemy tunnels to search and kill Viet Cong. The stress of his war experience left him with severe PTSD. His drug of choice was alcohol.

I HADN'T BEEN ON A motorcycle since the Spring of 1961. That was when "Caledonia," the bad boy of Princeton High, who my father forbade

me to date, took me for a spin on the back of his Ruby Red and Silver Tri-
umph. We rode out to a secluded field where I lost my "flower" to him – as
it turned out, in a sea of poison ivy. It was an unforgettable experience – in
many ways. Following this event, I ended up in the hospital for a severe
hemorrhagic ear infection. Much to my chagrin, the ugly, oozy, itchy rash
associated with poison ivy erupted in certain areas of my body where it
was not usually found. Luckily for me, the physicians on my ear infection
case were either truly puzzled or for the sake of a seventeen-year-old girl's
reputation, feigned ignorance.

Now here I was almost twenty years later, climbing on the back of
Dennis Casey's BMW, zipping through the streets of San Francisco; dodging the traffic and maneuvering the steep hills to buy art supplies or run
some menial errand. It was risky and exhilarating and I loved it. It got me
to thinking about what it might be like to own my own bike someday.

At the same time, Larry was having his own exciting adventure. Within
weeks of his arrival, he began to breathe life into the ailing Bradford enterprise. He came home every night animated and happy. It seemed for the
time being, as if our marriage and our personal lives had changed for the
better. We loved our house and we loved San Francisco. Larry still didn't
share much about his work with me, but as long as we were both thriving,
I believed we were in a good place.

Then one day this white stuff came over the top of Marin City and
smacked our house with dense fog and a wind that rocked the foundation.
It hung around for days, and then for weeks, and then for months. I wanted
to kill my real estate agent. She never told us that due to the angle of the
lot, this particular property got socked in while other houses around us
stayed completely in the clear. To say I was unhappy was putting it mildly.
Being fog bound for months at a time was not my idea of a California lifestyle. I toughed it out for a while before I became much too vocal about
it. I couldn't help myself, I was miserable. It turned into a droning plea to
Larry. "You're in the city, I'm at the Art Institute. We're both commuting.
The school Maida's in is really second rate. She could be better served
in a first-class school in San Francisco. Why are we doing this?" As usual,

whenever I brought up the subject, Larry stayed quiet, voicing no opinion one way or another.

Then finally in 1980, due to my constant nagging (or maybe Larry too, had grown tired of the fog and wind), we made the big move to the city. We bought an old, 1890s Victorian on Maple Street in the charming Presidio Heights neighborhood which was near parks and shopping and good schools. It was a classic Victorian as seen in all the tourist brochures, that had survived the great 1906 earthquake. Right away I began making plans on how to renovate it. Buying the house seemed like a financial stretch to me, but due to the severe recession at the time, the government was lending money to buyers and we were able to complete the sale. I was equally surprised when Larry put up no resistance to my remodeling plans. I imagined things were going well for him at work and as a result he had enough confidence in our financial situation to allow me the added expenditures. I had no clue as to what was really going on.

Word of Larry's successful rescue of the failing Bradford entity had spread through the tight-knit financial community. Reports of my husband as the new "wunderkind" had reached the ears of our Marin County real estate agent whose husband, Bill, worked at a burgeoning discount stock brokerage firm, Charles Schwab Corporation. He was able to introduce Larry to the founder and chairman, Chuck Schwab and his right-hand man, Hugo Quakenbush. Quakenbush knew that Chuck Schwab's strength was in promotion and marketing – he was an outside man – but not at his best in day-to-day operations. He needed a nuts-and-bolts guy like Larry. Chuck acknowledged that Larry's abilities were what he needed and hired him. Nearly a year to the day of his hiring, Larry officially became the first president of its Charles Schwab discount brokerage operation.

～

NO MATTER HOW WELL Larry was doing, he continued to look at our household expenses as his domain. I still had to hold my hand out for my bi-weekly allowance and account for every penny I spent. It was annoying, but I couldn't really hold it against him. Larry was a numbers guy. That was his big talent. Whereas I struggled to balance the checkbook, he could take one look at it and instantly spot the missing two cents. I always had confidence that no matter what other failings Larry might have as a husband, he would always be a good provider.

With Larry caught up in the expanding rigors of his work, the renovation of our stately Victorian fell mainly on my shoulders. Once again, I took on the job of project manager, but now found myself in a new city without any contacts in the construction world. I was at a loss for where to start. I mentioned my dilemma to our real estate agent and she said, "I know these two guys from Lake Tahoe, who are looking for some work. They're fun, they're talented. I'm sure they would come down and work with you." That sounded good to me.

A few days later the two guys showed up to give me an estimate on the cost of renovating the house. As advertised, they were fun and talented. What the real estate agent failed to mention was how drop-dead gorgeous they both were. They had those healthy outdoor looks that came from living an idyllic mountain lifestyle: skiing in the winter and doing construction work in the summer. The minute they walked in the door it was a done deal.

When demolition day came, Larry went off to work and Maida went off to school. There I was, left with these two handsome hunks, swinging their sledgehammers and gleefully ripping into the walls of my house. Oh, how I loved demo day!

One of the boys, the boss, was pretty serious-minded. The other one, his helper, Randy Odell, was more playful, and I could see he had his eye on me. I was looking pretty adorable myself at that time and as project manager I found lots of reasons to hang around. I justified my presence by saying I had to be there to sign the checks. I'd make myself useful by running some of their errands and fixing them lunch. In turn, they would teach me about plumbing and roofing. I actually did a lot of hands-on work and for a time we became like a little family. Eventually, all that working together in close quarters with the rippling muscles and glistening sweat became too much to handle. As you can imagine, Randy and I, well — one thing led to another. How we managed to find the time for physical intimacy I'll never know but we did, and it was extremely exciting. The sneaking around – no, I wasn't proud of that.

Lust is an amazing chemical. It makes you stupid. What else could have convinced us that this affair was our secret and nobody else would notice? Our relationship was so upsetting to Randy's boss, that he uninvited Randy from being the best man at his upcoming wedding. Then at some point it became clear that Larry was starting to sense something. One night in bed he questioned me and slammed his fists into the pillow out of frustration and anger. I lied through my teeth and he chose to believe me.

I loved Larry and even in the throes of my questionable behavior I never stopped working on our marriage or trying to find the scraps of connectivity that would hold us together. More than anything I wanted Maida to have a loving relationship with her father and for him to be part of her life. I remember having these marvelous chats with Maida over dinner while Larry worked late at the office. She was bright and articulate and could describe in perfect detail the interactions she had at school with her friends and teachers. Like me, she loved learning and was excited about every new discovery she made. When Larry got home, I would say, "Maida, tell Dad what your day was like." She dutifully would repeat the stories of her school day while Larry listened with half an ear. Finally, one day she said, "Mom, I don't want to do that anymore. I don't want to be repeating myself. If Dad can't be home in time for dinner, sorry that's too bad." I was trying to make us a family, but she wasn't playing along. The truth was Maida and Larry interacted with each other out of obligation and I had to accept their definition of a father-daughter relationship.

Somewhere in the back of my brain, the troubling notion that Larry and I might not be together for the rest of our lives began to creep in. The very idea frightened me. As I often did with unpleasant things, I tried to put it out of my mind. Maybe if I didn't think about it, it would go away. Like Scarlett O'Hara in *Gone with the Wind*, I would "think about it tomorrow."

CHAPTER 10

Finding My Way

1982

The Tahoe boys finished the demolition and some of the reconstruction; sheet rock, plumbing, electrics, and roofing. Once they were gone, things began to calm down. Our marriage resumed some sense of normalcy and I moved on to the finer details of painting, cabinetmaking, and wallpaper. For this phase of the renovation, I hired experienced contractors including a very interesting couple who designed and manufactured all my cabinets. Besides their high-quality carpentry business, they owned a small art gallery and were very impressed with my artwork. Because they had good taste I appreciated their opinion. Their comments came at a crucial time when I was struggling to find my artistic direction.

Imagine my excitement when a few months later the couple who had done my cabinetry offered to give me a one-woman show at their gallery in San Francisco. Frankly, I had no idea of what to expect. My only previous gallery experience had been in Connecticut in group shows with my fellow students, attended mostly by local residents who were eager to show their support of struggling artists. Showing in an art gallery in San Francisco was an altogether different experience. In San Francisco, there were hundreds of small galleries and thousands of artists. Getting attention for your one-woman show meant elbowing your way into an already overcrowded marketplace. It was costly and time consuming. My body of work from the Art

Institute was limited, so I decided to include some of the paintings I had done at the thread factory in Connecticut. No matter how much we promoted the event, my one-woman show was attended mostly by my friends from the Art Institute, the Schwab world, and parents of Maida's friends. I remember the husband of one of my girlfriends leaning over to her and saying, "Why are we here?"

Basically, the gallery opening in San Francisco consisted of offering wine and cheese and saying to friends, "Will you buy my artwork?" I found it depressing. One of my paintings did sell to a stranger. It was a really good painting I had done when we were living in Westport. The guy who bought it thought it was amazing. As he walked off with it all I could think was, "Well, I'll never see that again." The few dollars in my hand didn't make up for the profound feeling of embarrassment – after all the effort it took to make this show happen, what came out of it was the sale of a single painting.

While at the Art Institute, I was involved with a few more gallery shows. It was a lot of work putting these shows together and I always thought that the artists were the least important people in the room. For the most part, I felt it was a racket. I watched my fellow artists being ripped off left, right and center by so-called art dealers who took sixty percent of whatever you sold and you supplied the hors d'oeuvres and wine. The friends who came were primarily other starving artists. By the time I finished art school, I'd pretty much had it with gallery shows.

BY 1981, LARRY'S CAREER was skyrocketing. When it was formally announced in the financial news that Larry Stupski had been hired by Charles Schwab as President and COO, it was a big feather in Larry's cap. I knew the fancy title must have come with a big salary bump, but that information was never divulged to me. Even though we were now living in very comfortable circumstances, able to afford most everything we wanted, Larry continued to hold on tight to the purse strings. Under that feathered cap, he was still the poor boy from a cinderblock house in Jacksonville, Florida, haunted by the fear of failure and holding on to every dollar.

I, on the other hand, was dealing with my own troubling view of the art world. I was surrounded by impoverished artists but I didn't have that worry. I hid my financial stability as much as I could because I never wanted anybody to think I was a frustrated housewife dabbling in art. I often felt like an outsider which made me truly grateful for my friendship with Dennis Casey. We never hid anything from each other. Dennis and I shared our most personal stories, including him telling me about a brief homosexual encounter he once had. We could tell each other anything without fear of being judged. We were "best friends."

Eventually I did find a few like-minded women artists who were also financially secure, either by marriage or because they were already working in the commercial art world. We had a lot in common and we developed a group that got together to commiserate about everything from finding a good housekeeper to what a lousy deal women had in the art world. We couldn't help but notice that almost all the male artists had wives raising their kids and putting dinner on the table while the female artists were expected to do it all. We were feminists, whether we self-identified as such or not, and we were experiencing those frustrations and inequalities that would manifest as a full-blown Women's Rights movement.

In 1983, my graduation from the Art Institute coincided with another life-changing event, one that nearly eclipsed the joy of receiving my diploma. Prior to my graduation date, I accompanied Larry to Los Angeles to attend a Schwab conference at the posh Bel Air Hotel. That night after the formal Schwab dinner, as we lay side by side in bed enjoying the plush comfort of our luxurious suite, Larry decided it was the right time to let me know he was having an affair.

I don't know what prompted Larry to tell me that shattering news. Maybe it was the fact that I was popular with his co-workers. They had made a fuss over me at dinner and it may have made him jealous. Further, he announced, that when we got back to San Francisco he was moving out. He had already found himself a bachelor pad a couple of blocks away from our Victorian. I was more than devastated. I was a basket case. I remember crying my eyes out.

I had made arrangements for a friend from Connecticut, Pam Williams, to come out to San Francisco and do a girls' trip with me up and down the coast of California. She was quite a talented artist who had been a fellow student at the thread factory in Westport. She knew Larry from the Connecticut years and when I told her what had happened, she was pretty confident Larry would come back. I was not so sure. I had had an affair, which I never fessed up to. Unlike Larry, I felt my transgression was my burden to bear and I would go to my grave with it. Even the Catholic girl in me said there were good reasons to lie at times.

The day I walked across the stage to accept my diploma I was filled with mixed emotions -- satisfaction at having achieved my goal and a profound sadness about my personal life. My great pride at becoming the first female in our family to achieve a four-year degree was completely diminished by my mother who didn't see my earning a BFA as enough of an accomplishment for her and my father to attend the celebration in person. The only positive aspect of their not coming was that it would delay having to let them know that Larry and I had separated. As I looked out into the audience, the only friendly face I could see was twelve-year-old Maida. Her genuine smile lifted my spirits. Next to her sat Larry stoically, showing no signs of emotion. He may not have taken any pride in my accomplishment, but at least he was there saving me from the embarrassment of having to explain to my teachers and classmates why my husband had not attended. When the graduation was over, Maida and I went home to our Victorian house on Maple Street and Larry went to his bachelor pad.

I LEFT THE ART INSTITUTE WITHOUT much of a portfolio. Even so, I had no problem graduating. The Art Institute's criteria was based on the fact that they'd been involved in my artistic development for five years. My professors recognized that I had talent and had taken my work at the Institute seriously. I earned my diploma with flying colors. But once I graduated, I had no idea of what to do or how I would translate what I had learned into something meaningful and fulfilling.

As it turned out, my friend Pam's prediction had been correct. After a few excruciating weeks, Larry found an excuse for us to get together and "talk things out." Somehow, between the two of us, he was convinced to end the affair. A few days later he moved back into Maple Street. That night we held on to each other tightly and made love more passionately than we had in a long time. In the momentary pleasure, we once again believed in the possibility of our future happiness.

I HAD CREATED A SMALL studio space in the attic of our Victorian house, but as my artistic ideas developed it proved to be a less than ideal situation. I knew I wanted to explore on a bigger canvas and I needed some space to stretch out. One weekend, when Larry was out of town on business, I got a call from the cabinetmaker and his wife who had given me the one-woman show.

"Hey Linda, we thought of you because a space just opened up in the building next to our carpentry shop. It would make a perfect art studio and we wondered if you might be interested."

I hadn't considered setting up a separate studio for my work, but their offer intrigued me. I went to take a look. The space was in Bayview, one of the lowest income neighborhoods in San Francisco. It had once been home to a thriving naval shipyard and shipbuilding facilities. The deindustrialization of the district in the 1970s and 1980s had resulted in increased unemployment and local poverty levels. Rents were dirt cheap. The studio was only $30 a month plus it was a good size space – big enough to hold numerous large canvases. I decided to take it, despite the drawback that it had once been the tannery for a nearby slaughterhouse and still maintained a distinct aroma of its former incarnation.

When Larry learned I had taken a studio space, he was furious. The higher Larry rose in the financial world the less tolerance he had for things he could not control. The fact that I took on an expenditure – no matter how small – without consulting him was enough to inflame him. There was more to his anger than just the cost of the studio. The fact that I now had a space of my own meant there was a part of my life that was free from his influence. I could feel his growing resentment.

Over the past year he had made some particularly spiteful comments about my artistic pursuits. On one occasion, he took the opportunity to remind me I was already $50,000 in debt for art school.

The real zinger came the night Larry and I were out for dinner with a really lovely couple we had known in Connecticut. As often happens with couples, the girls were talking to each other and the guys were talking to each other. I was going on about how I had just graduated from the Art Institute and that I was the first woman in my family to earn a college degree. My friend was so excited for me she stopped and looked over to Larry and said, "Oh, Larry, you must be so proud of Linda." Larry flushed, his skin actually turned bright red. He was so stymied he couldn't respond and the three of us looked at him like "What the heck's happening here?" Finally, he blurted out, "Lots of people go to college." I was crushed. It was such a dismissive comment that it left no doubt in anyone's mind how Larry felt about my achievements.

~~~

ONE OF THE FIRST THINGS I discovered when I moved into my new studio was how alone I was. My teachers were gone, my accomplishments had been poo-pooed by Larry, and I had no supportive environment. It was just me. I had nobody to schmooze and laugh with. I put up a hammock and curled up in it and cried every day for six weeks, wondering what I was going to come up with. Then one day I picked up a book on Picasso and somewhere in that book he said, "People always ask me 'How does this happen? Do you plan these kinds of things that you make?'" His answer was, "No, the best part is I never know what's going to happen. That's what appeals to me, and that's how it happens."

It struck me like a thunderbolt. "That's me!" I thought, "I'm stuck on thinking I have to know what I am doing – like in my nursing, where you do A, you do B, you do C. It's all formula. But you couldn't apply that to art. When Picasso said, "The best part is, I don't know what's going to happen," it completely made sense to me. Now, my dreaded question of "What am I going to come up with?" was filled with the wonder and anticipation of discovery.

I wiped my tears and got out my black and white paints. I had this ratty piece of canvas I had saved because I was a "leftover" girl. (My mother used to wash off the aluminum foil. Do you remember those days?) And suddenly I knew I had to do a self-portrait. I held up a mirror in one hand and a paint brush in the other and began applying paint to canvas. I was pleased with how much control of my technique I had. I began in one corner of the canvas, looked in the mirror and started painting – back and forth – mirror, painting, mirror, painting, until the portrait was done. I stood back to admire my handiwork and was pleased with what I saw. Best of all, it came so effortlessly. I had been freed. I closed my eyes and said a "thanks" to Pablo Picasso.

⁓

I WAS STILL EXPERIMENTING ARTISTICALLY, and it took me a while to get a handle on which medium was right for me. Each medium has its own challenge and every artist has to find their comfort zone. When you're an oil painter, you're married to the oils. The oils have position; they have influence. You're negotiating with that oil paint all the time. Acrylics are the worst, they have more say than I want. They dry faster than I want, they don't show the color the way I want, and they don't have the life of oil paint which is real pigment. But drawing – that's a different story. When you're drawing, you're completely in charge. The medium doesn't have a say. It's all up to you. It took me a while to figure that out. But once I discovered that I had a certain flow with charcoal and pastels and an eraser, that I could make something happen, that I could be in total control, I thought, "This is where I belong. This suits my way of getting an image to reveal itself." That was a big breakthrough for me. Finally, I began to create a style that was truly my own.

The next thing I did was buy a gigantic roll of paper. I stapled it across the top to a beam and let it fall to the bottom. Then I cut off a number of huge pieces of paper that were inviting me to do something. I developed a ritual. Before I would even start to work I would sweep the floor, have a cigarette, and a cup of coffee. Sometimes I would catch up on some magazines or listen to the news on the radio. I would start playing what music I was going to listen to. I had a lot of cassette tapes. Eventually, one would grab my attention. I'd look around and think, what do I do now? I remember walking to this one corner where I had a large piece of paper laid out and I did something, I don't know if I erased something or I placed the pastel down on the paper. But the second it happened something inside said to me, "You were always going to do that, right then, at that moment. You just didn't know it." I thought, "It starts with a mark. That's all I have to do is start with a mark," then depending on my mood, my aesthetics, my pep or lack thereof, and music, especially if it was Mozart, I would just go for it. I would do — stuff. Turn it around; work vertically rather than horizontally, or vice versa. Wake it up with an eraser until I'd start to see something happen. Then I would home in on it. I would go back with the black charcoal and select things that meant something to me visually. One day I was on a roll when something truly strange occurred. I kind of blacked out for God knows how long and when I "woke up" I was bent over in front of this big drawing and I kept hearing this howl and it was coming from me. I thought, oh my God what just happened? I had no idea how long I'd been in that state but I had a finished piece of artwork that I don't remember making. It was big, 60" x 80". The image was a U-shaped door cracked open with a sliver of bright light. That's all it was. I have no idea how I entered that creative space or how I achieved that work of art and it never happened to me again, but as a result, something inside me changed. I had reached a point where it didn't matter what I did. It just didn't matter.

CHAPTER 11

Goddess Camp

1985

What would you think about your mom getting a motorcycle? That was the question I put to my twelve-year-old daughter. It was something Dennis Casey and I had discussed off and on ever since I expressed my love for the freedom and excitement I experienced on his bike. "Mom, no!" Maida cringed. "I'd be so embarrassed in front of my friends!" The last thing I wanted to do was embarrass my daughter. I let the matter go – for the time being. But picturing myself on my own motorcycle was never far from my mind.

Besides the physical joy of riding a motorcycle, I got strength from being myself. "This is who I am. Take it or leave it." Larry, despite his college hijinks, had settled into the role of a buttoned-down president and COO of a major financial institution. Obviously, I was not the typical corporate wife.

We were once invited to a Schwab event at the Treasury Building in downtown San Francisco. As usual Larry was working late, so we planned to meet there. I threw on this great looking turtleneck with a slim leather skirt and a pair of Neiman Marcus high leather boots my sister bought me that were decorated with spurs. They didn't have the sharp spikes like real spurs, but they had the chain and the part that went under your heel. They were pretty spiffy. I came waltzing into this cocktail party jingling my spurs and right away all heads turned in my direction, including Chuck Schwab who looked me up and down and said, "Yep it's Linda!"

All the attention I got didn't sit well with Larry. You'd like to think a husband's response would be, "She's so unique. How great. I'm proud she's mine." But no, that wasn't his reaction. He didn't like the fact that I was admired. It was almost as if any admiration directed at me diminished his own status. He couldn't tolerate that and never failed to point out how inane or inappropriate my behavior was. I had my own issues of self-worth and Larry's stinging criticism was soul crushing. It began to feel like he was throwing a wet blanket over everything I did. I still wanted our marriage to work and struggled to put on a happy face, but inside I felt I was dying.

One day my manicurist, who I had taken into my confidence, told me about something she thought might be of interest to me. It was called Goddess Camp, a Northern California retreat where women gathered to explore their inner lives. That got my attention, and in early 1987 I signed up, along with 299 other women, to attend one week of Goddess Camp at Harbin Hot Springs, a spiritually oriented retreat center located thirty minutes north of the Napa Valley wine region.

My father had come for a visit to attend a Schwab golf tournament with Larry. On the day I left for Goddess Camp, as I said goodbye to the two most important men in my life, my knees began to shake. Was it a foreboding that I was about to embark on a dangerous journey? I was keenly aware that I was heading into an experience that might somehow change me. It was an unnerving feeling that stayed with me on the long drive. When I finally arrived at Goddess Camp, the "welcome circle" had already enclosed. Upon seeing me, two women broke hands and welcomed me in. Despite their warm greeting, I could not help but think about bolting back to the imagined security of the two men I had left behind. After the evening meal and fire pit, I decided to make a bed on the ground next to my car. As I clambered to pull out my sleeping bag, I caught sight of some hair my dog had shed on the back seat of the car. It stirred such a profound sense of longing and homesickness that I burst into tears. It wasn't until a day later, in a mask making group, that I began to feel a sense of belonging.

Could there have been any woman who came to the camp more in need of emotional support than me? I doubt it.

Goddess Camp was everything I hoped for. It had all the benefits of a wonderful summer camp: lounging on the docks of the local swimming hole, great meals, lectures, arts and crafts, and a spiritual component which included chanting, drumming, and the opportunity to just let loose. Women of all ages and all walks of life were part of the diverse community, and the mandate was to be totally yourself without fear of judgment. Listening to the other women speak about their lives made me realize I wasn't too needy (as Larry often claimed), I wasn't crazy, and I wasn't alone. My lifetime of self-inflicted reprisals began to fall away like blocks of concrete. By the end of the week, I felt as if I had been set free. The fear I encountered when I said goodbye to Larry and Dod no longer had a hold on me. I came home renewed, energized, and in touch with my true self. I knew I would return to Goddess Camp the following year.

Larry must have noticed the profound change that had taken place in me and I don't think he liked what he saw. But it didn't matter; there was no going back. I was becoming the Linda I always wanted to be.

SOMETIMES, IN A DESPERATE attempt to save a marriage a couple will take an exotic trip or have a baby or buy a new house. In 1987 Larry and I decided to purchase a big, beautiful, expensive home in San Francisco's posh Presidio Terrace neighborhood. Part of Larry's job included entertaining clients and we would often give intimate dinner parties, which I enjoyed hosting. The Maple Street Victorian had its charm, but the Presidio Terrace house offered a much more impressive setting and was far more suited to Larry's prestigious position at Schwab.

Presidio Terrace was a neighborhood filled with the rich and famous, including then mayor, Dianne Feinstein, who lived across the street, and further down the block, Nancy Pelosi, the newly elected member of the U.S. House of Representatives – two powerful women who were role models for many of their peers.

No sooner did we move in that I began a make-over project. The house was in great shape but needed some updating, especially in the master bedroom and bath where I wanted all new appliances, a walk-in closet for two, and additional living space. Larry didn't seem to have any objections to the sizeable price tag for the renovations. I figured if we could afford the house we could certainly afford the remodel. With Dennis Casey's help, I began knocking down walls and purchasing building materials.

Shortly after we took ownership the stock market crashed.

Charles Schwab & Co., the nation's largest discount brokerage, sustained a one-day loss of $22 million in the market's plunge, largely because one customer, a wealthy Hong Kong investor, could not meet the margin calls – a requirement that he put up additional cash to cover the declining value of his stock portfolio. As word of those losses spread, Schwab's stock skidded and opened on Monday down 60% from its offering price.

What that meant or what that would look like in the future, no one knew, but we all knew it wasn't good. It was a shock to our immediate family and to the entire Charles Schwab company. Because of the fifteen-hour time difference between Hong Kong and San Francisco, Larry was pretty much at it 24 hours a day. And he was ashen. I mean he was looking awful. Other famous brokerages were going under, sending shock waves through the financial world. It looked as if the whole market was on the brink of collapse. I felt totally helpless but tried my best to give Larry whatever support he needed. Was it cuddles and hugs or just to let him have his space? Whatever it was, I wanted him to know that when the chips were down, I was there for him.

It took months before Schwab was able to regain their footing. I have no idea how they did it, but I'm sure Larry was a key player in figuring out how the company would survive. In fact, it wouldn't surprise me at all if he was responsible for crafting whatever brilliant solution pulled them back from the edge.

When the cloud finally lifted, I took it upon myself to call Helen Schwab and a few other executive wives. They were all in terrible condition. It had been terrifying for them to watch the lives and fortunes of those around them crumble overnight. Helen thanked me for picking up the phone and revealed how frightening it had been for her and Chuck. She was very kind and grateful that I had reached out. At some point, when we could finally start breathing again and things started to get back to normal, I said to Larry, "I think everyone in the company needs to get together and I don't think Helen's up to having any kind of gathering. How about we do it?"

Other firms like Merrill Lynch, were constantly throwing big parties where the executives would have to schmooze with this guy, that guy, this client, that client. That just never happened at Schwab. Unlike lots of corporations, Chuck discouraged employee social gatherings that were unrelated to work. But now it seemed the right thing to do, to bring everyone together to recognize what we had all been through and how we had all survived. I think the idea appealed to Larry because it gave him an opportunity to show off our beautiful new home. He agreed.

Our big fancy kitchen and the overall layout of the house were particularly conducive for entertaining. I had no idea how to throw a big party – it was never my thing, but fortunately all my experience as a project manager came in handy. With the help of some caterers, I figured it all out and it was truly wonderful. Everybody came. At one point, Helen took me aside and said, "It was really nice of you to do this. We all needed it." She was right. It was a healing experience for everyone.

IN 1988, I COULDN'T WAIT to get back to Goddess Camp. There was no resistance from Larry. By now he had gotten used to the idea that I was going to do what I was going to do, so there wasn't even a discussion about it. I returned to camp filled with excitement and anticipation. There were quite a few faces I recognized from the previous year but also many new ones. One young woman caught my interest because she came rumbling in late at night on an old Yamaha motorcycle, even though she'd had a couple of mechanical breakdowns along the way. Even with those difficulties, she'd figured out how to get herself there. I remember being told that she slowly poked into camp in the dark. The dirt roads were unmarked and the road signs were sparse, yet she somehow found the entrance and decided rather than wake up the rest of us with this clunky old motorcycle, she would lie down beside it in her sleeping bag, similar to what I had done the year before. I was impressed with her story and made a point of meeting her. I told her about my affinity for motorcycles and how brave I thought she was to have made the trip. She accepted my comments graciously and offered to take me for a ride on the back of her bike. I accepted.

The following afternoon we left camp and with my arms wrapped tightly around her waist we rode up, down, and around the tree-lined hills and roads. She was a confident rider and managed the throbbing bike with such authority that I was able to relax and give myself over to the amazing experience. By the end of the ride, I had become infatuated and was absolutely bowled over by the feelings I had for her.

Aesthetically, she was nothing that I would have looked at twice in any other situation. It had to do with the freedom that she had and this pioneer spirit that got her to drive a motorcycle to the camp all on her own. I was ripe for some sort of explosion of female power, but my overpowering attraction to her was baffling. I never saw it coming.

I didn't dare mention my mad "girl crush" to anyone, but I had an aching heart and it kept me awake at night. I was pining for her and it was shocking to me because I never had an experience like that before. Finally, at the end of the week when we all were getting ready to go home I got up the nerve to say something. I went to her and I opened up my heart and she gently took me under her wing and said, "You go back home. Just live your life the way you've been doing. I'm flattered and appreciative and I think you're an amazing person, but this is not what you want." She was tender and sweet and her way of handling it was so empathetic that I thought, "She knows more about this than I do." I admired her even more. Later that day, I watched her ride off on her bike and knew I would probably never see her again, but she had given me a gift that would stay with me forever – she had opened up another piece of my heart.

The last evening of Goddess Camp is celebrated around a huge bonfire and it's a final chance for anyone who so desires to get up and perform.

One at a time the women recite a poem, or dance, or sing, or do anything to express their emotions. Without ever thinking about it, I jumped up and said, "I just want you all to know that I've made a big decision this week." I paused for dramatic effect – they always loved a bit of drama – and when I saw I had everyone's attention I announced loud and clear, "I'm coming back next year and I'm coming back on a motorcycle." The place erupted; everyone was hooting and hollering. I hadn't quite expected such an enthusiastic response and I thought, "Oh wow, I'm really gonna' have to do this."

When my turn was over two young women approached me and said, "This is so amazing, we're so happy for you and we want to tell you, when you come back to camp next year we'll be waiting in the parking lot when you ride in." That sealed the deal. I knew that what I had to do in the coming year was learn to ride a motorcycle. But there was one hurdle to overcome before I put my plan in motion.

When I came back from Goddess Camp I sat down with Maida and said, "You're seventeen, you're graduating high school, you're ready to be launched into your life. Can we discuss this idea of mom getting a bike again?" And she said, "Of course. I have no problem with that." Just like that it was over. I had no more excuses.

CHAPTER 12

BMW Linda

1989

One afternoon in my art studio I mentioned my brief Goddess Camp infatuation to Dennis. I thought he would be very understanding because he was more fluid in his sexuality. Much to my surprise, he looked askance at me when I told him about my crush and I never spoke about it again to anybody. The truly important take-away from Goddess Camp was the assignment I had given myself. If there's one thing I know about myself, it's that I'm true to my word. When I make a promise, I feel honor bound to keep it. I knew those two women would be waiting for me next year to come rolling into camp on my motorcycle and I intended to do just that.

Within a week or two after Goddess Camp, I was at the DMV getting my permit. In California, they had a program where they hired a company to give you motorcycle lessons. I signed up without a second thought. A group of guys had developed this motorcycle training school and they had these short Honda motorcycles that looked like small Harleys. They were pretty low to the ground so that most of us would be able to keep flat-footed which is a big help when you're starting out. The first lesson you don't even turn the engine on, you just push along like a kid on a scooter. You straddled the bike, the instructor led, and we followed along like little ducklings. That got us used to the feel of the bike. My first thought was "Oh my gosh! This thing is heavier than I thought." We were in charge of keeping our bikes upright and that didn't always happen because if you made too tight a turn you'd just go "bonk" off to the side and that's when you'd realize how heavy those things were. The lessons were about an hour a day for five days. They had us going around cones and making stops using signals and there was a test at the end, which I easily passed.

Once I had my learner's permit, Dennis and I decided to purchase a small Honda motorcycle like the one I had trained on. I was proud to be the owner of my very own bike, but for some reason, once I had it I just didn't get on it. Was it fear? Lack of interest? Who knows? I just wasn't motivated to take it for a ride. The truth is I was scared to death!

There was a garage at our house in Presidio Terrace underneath the kitchen. I parked the bike there and there it sat. Dennis was doing some handyman work for me on the house and one day he came up from the garage and said "You know what I could do with that bike? Simple solution. I'll take off the gas tank, I'll drain it and I'll clean it up and turn it into a planter!" I said "Okay, Dennis, I get it." The following Sunday I decided by hook or by crook, I was going to spend some time on that motorcycle.

The next street over from Presidio Terrace is Lake Street. It runs for about twenty blocks and dead ends at Lincoln Park. I figured that was about as much of a trip as I could handle and that I would take the bike out in the morning while people were in church and the streets were quiet. That "maiden voyage" was intense because your hands and feet are all learning to do something new at the same time. You've got the hand brake and the throttle and the clutch and the footbrake and you have to get deep into the coordination quickly because messing up any one of those four things can kill you.

That first ride involved one stop sign which I managed to get across – doing about ten miles an hour while thinking I'm doing forty. I came to a smooth stop and didn't lay the bike down at any point in the ride. When I finally made it back home, I literally plunked myself down and went straight to bed. My hands ached, my feet ached, my ankles hurt, and I was just grateful I made it back in one piece.

I became comfortable on the Honda pretty quickly and in typical Linda fashion, before long, I found myself totally engaged in the world of motorcycling. At that very first training course where I got my permit, I remember one of the teachers saying, "There are usually three reasons people get a motorcycle. One it's the cheapest mode of transportation, two is that somebody in their life is trying to push them into getting their own license, and the third reason is you get the "disease." I'm the one who got the "disease." Hook, line, and sinker.

I totally immersed myself in the world of bikes. I was completely enamored of these fabulous machines and became aware of opportunities to better my handling and increase my enjoyment and survival skills. Eventually, I signed up for day-long courses taught by the best trainers at Laguna Seca Raceway in Salinas, California, and Sears Point in Sonoma County, California (now known as Sonoma Raceway). The skills the instructors emphasized were super smooth gear changes, the correct angle of the bike on corners and tips for not being in the wrong place at the wrong time.

To practice for the final DMV skills test, I developed a route from Presidio Terrace (with a stop at the Bay Club Fitness Center for stretch/step classes) to my art studio at the dead end of Revere Street in The Bayview. It was about ten to twelve miles one way and gave me a variety of traffic experiences: congestion, traffic/stop lights, crazy intersections, cable car/railway tracks, and wooden road surfaces with gaps on the Lefty O'Doul Bridge.

After a few months, I was feeling ready for a bigger challenge. Larry and I were scheduled to go to a YPO (Young Presidents' Organization) meeting in Woodside, California. At the last minute, there was some emergency at Schwab. Chuck Schwab had to be at the YPO meeting and both of them couldn't be away from the office, so Larry drew the short straw. He knew that I was looking forward to going to Woodside and said, "I can't make it but it's up to you if you want to go." I said, "Yeah, I'll take my bike." By now, whatever opinion Larry had of my biker life, he kept to himself. To me it was another indication that he had become emotionally detached and didn't care one way or the other what I did.

Woodside is a small community about forty-five minutes south of San Francisco, near Palo Alto. It's filled with beautiful oaks and redwoods and is reached by a scenic winding road, Skyline Boulevard. It seemed like a perfect chance to stretch out and use my new riding skills. I was now experienced enough to recognize that the throbbing you feel between your legs when you get on a bike is a power that will take you anywhere you want to go. For me it was a power I had been lacking in my life. Whatever fears I would have to face and however long it would take me to gain control of that power, I knew it would all be worth it because in that struggle to gain control I would find my true self.

That's where my head was at when I decided to make the solo trip to Woodside. Once I set out, it was a lot further than I thought. The forty-three miles seemed to take forever and it was so cold my teeth were chattering all through the drive along Skyline Boulevard. Fortunately, as soon as I dropped down towards Palo Alto, it warmed up, and by the time I reached the meeting site it felt like a regular spring day and I was feeling that rare sense of freedom and exhilaration that motorcycling offers.

I pulled into the parking lot where some of the YPO guys were milling around. I had on a really good-looking outfit and when I took off my motorcycle gear they just dropped their mouths, "Linda?" As it turned out, a lot of them were motorcyclists. All the girls were saying, "Oh my God, Linda, this is fabulous. When did this happen?" It was another pat on the back and frankly I was completely surprised at how many motorcycle owners there were in the YPO network that I didn't know about. I'm sure that reports of my arrival in Woodside got back to Larry, but he never said one word about it. I had no way of knowing whether he admired my new-found passion or was jealous of it. Then one morning Larry and I were heading out to another Schwab event and as we were leaving Larry stopped on the staircase, turned around to me and said, "Could you just not be the star today?" That told me everything I needed to know.

After the trip to Woodside, I gained confidence in my bike riding ability and decided I wanted to be on a taller bike because it gave you an advantage in traffic. Dennis found a listing in a motorcycle magazine for a 1965 BMW R65, a beautiful German bike with classic lines. Dennis was dead set on me having a BMW because of the safety factor of the design. The fact that it had two cylinders that stick out on the side meant that if you ever went down, those cylinders would keep you from being pinned under the bike and would prevent your leg from being burned or squashed. That sounded good to me. Dennis went to Texas, bought the bike, and rode it back to San Francisco. I loved it! It was a thing of beauty. It was blue and sleek – the antithesis of the Harley hog which automatically separated BMW riders into a very different category of bike enthusiasts. Now it felt like I was on a real bike.

The kid who lived next door also had a BMW and every weekend we would go out riding together. One of the joys of biking was that a forty-year-old woman and a seventeen-year-old boy could be linked together by their mutual love of a machine and become peers regardless of age.

Sometimes Dennis took me out to help me practice. He'd say, "Come on, let's just go over to Oakland," or, "Let's go over to Berkeley." We'd go across the bridge and do all the exits and grab a bite to eat and turn around and come back. On my own I'd go up into the hills above 19th Avenue and just follow my nose. I'd do elevations, downhills, learning how to stop at a moment's notice; stop on a hill, get going on a hill, and put myself in situations where I was always challenging my skill level.

By now I was becoming competent and getting serious. I was taking good courses and reading every motorcycle magazine I could get my hands on. I was getting a real kick out of turning myself into a biker chick, riding my own classy machine. At the beginning, men treated me differently than their fellow motorcyclists and I had to learn how to cut that off at the pass. One of my more annoying conversations would be a guy coming up to me after we'd been riding for a while wanting to help me with my bike, which you don't do without permission. It was something he would never do to a man. I remember being with Dennis at one point when we ran into a couple of his buddies and right away he went up to them and said, "Listen, I want you to know she's a real biker." That helped a lot.

During this time, I was very influenced by all these amazing motor-cycle trips Dennis did with his buddies and how he always came back with fun stories about people they ran into, side roads they didn't expect to take, and weather conditions they had to overcome. It seemed exciting, unlike anything I'd ever done and it just kept building up inside me. I was ready for the next big challenge.

Coincidently, underneath my studio, there was a BMW motorcycle repair shop. This is where Dennis and I would hang out with Dave, who was the BMW motorcycle mechanic. It was a great spot to just talk bikes. One day a young woman named Karen Armstrong came in with her bike and mentioned that she wanted to go on a bike trip to Mexico. Dennis had traveled a lot in Mexico and she asked his advice on where to go. This was 1989 and she was a woman traveling by herself so Dennis told her not to go to the mainland, but to go to Baja because it was a sleepy, quiet, safer place. Then out of the blue I asked her if she would mind if I came along. She had always traveled by herself and at first, she wasn't sure it was a good idea but finally she said, "Sure, let's do it." Just like that my first road trip fell into my lap.

It was in March, during St. Patrick's week. My daughter Maida was going to be on spring break from high school and she had made plans with her friends. Larry didn't express any concern over my going, so for him it was a non-event. It wasn't as if I didn't recognize the potential dangers of the trip. I knew that I was going to be pretty much disconnected from anyone who could come to my rescue and I decided that if we had any prob-lems along the way the one person I could call would be Dennis.

The day I left, I was as scared as I had ever been and was questioning my sanity – "I'm a mother of a seventeen-year-old. Why am I doing this? I don't know anything about Karen. There are all kinds of hazards. Is this just another crazy impulse?" I felt a panic begin to set in; a trembling, much like the day when I left Dod and Larry to go to Goddess Camp. But within a few blocks of taking off, my nerves began to calm down and by the time I met Karen at the agreed upon spot in the Army Street parking lot, I knew I was in it for good and there was no turning back.

CHAPTER 13

Lost in Tijuana

1989

Karen and I set our itinerary. We'd go down Highway 101 from San Francisco and make a stop in Santa Barbara. I had made arrangements for us to stay with Kathy Araujo, a friend who Larry, Maida, and I had met on a vacation in Mexico. The trip from San Francisco to Santa Barbara was a breeze until we got stopped for speeding just north of Santa Barbara. It was my fault. I was in front. The cop never said a word to us. Took our licenses, gave us tickets, and drove off. Karen and I limped off the next exit and went and got a piece of pie. It was the first glitch in what had so far been a perfect trip. In truth, it was no big deal and the next morning we got an early start and headed down to the Tijuana border around 8:00 a.m. The trip was uneventful until we hit L.A. where we got stuck in bumper-to-bumper traffic.

The first thing I had to learn was how to keep my hands from cramping. You've got clutches and throttles and when you're in slow traffic it's a lot of mini movements that can wear you out quickly, so motorcyclists have figured out ways to keep moving. Fortunately, Karen was a good teacher and taught me how to "split lanes," which means riding between stopped cars. It's a practice which while not exactly legal is tolerated in California due to motorcycle motors overheating in stop-and-go traffic.

The rule is you only go five miles an hour faster than the traffic is going. So, if the traffic is stopped or slowed you can keep moving ahead but only at five to ten miles an hour. You can always see cops on bikes doing the same thing.

Once the traffic starts to move, you can adjust your speed and at some point go right back into line with everybody else. Karen didn't have to explain everything; she just came up alongside me and said, "Are you ready to follow me?" I said, "Okay," and just like that she showed me how to split lanes and we got out of that L.A. mess.

Karen taught me a lot of different things about being a biker, like if your kickstand started to sink to look around for a can or rock to stick under it. She also pointed out that men have strength in their upper body which aids in moving their bikes, but women have their strength from their waist down and showed me how to lean the bike on a hip in order to walk it forward or backwards into a better position – tips that guys didn't tell me because they couldn't relate to it. As it turned out, this trip would be a learning experience in many ways.

It was lunchtime when we stopped in San Diego. We decided to grab a bite to eat before we crossed the border at San Ysidro. The plan was to take the road toward Rosarito and head down to Ensenada, a pretty beach town about fifty miles south of Tijuana. Once we had taken care of business at the border – paperwork, money exchange, insurance – it was only 3:30 pm; plenty of time to get to Ensenada where we would spend the night. We had been warned that the road got a bit confusing on the Mexican side and once we got through the border that's when things went wrong. Instead of heading towards Rosarito, we found ourselves heading into Tijuana. Karen saw our error in time and was able to correct her course. She was a better and more experienced biker. I was afraid to make the sudden move and kept going straight ahead. When I couldn't see her anywhere I knew I was in trouble. I got off at the next exit and ended up in the thickest, ugliest part of Tijuana with no idea of how to get back to the freeway. Fortunately, I spotted a police car and they directed me back towards a freeway entrance. I found my way to the onramp but nothing about the road looked like the highway we had been on, so I did a quick exit and headed back towards town on a road that ran parallel to the highway. Halfway back to town, who do I spot but Karen, on the highway going in the opposite direction. Obviously, she was looking for me. We waved at each other and I figured the best thing was to stay put so that one of us was stationary. I hoped she might make the same U-turn I did but after waiting twenty minutes and seeing three motorcycles pass by, none of them Karen, I decided to share my plight with a couple of policemen who at first assured me that my "amiga" would show up soon. Eventually they recognized as I did that Karen wasn't coming back. They spoke with some other policemen and learned one of them had seen a woman on a BMW. They never said where but they instructed me to follow their car. Several blocks and a lot of traffic later, it was obvious that Karen was nowhere to be found. The cops then suggested that I follow them into downtown Tijuana where she might be looking for me. I followed them for what seemed like hours. Later, they saw that I was exhausted and suggested that I hop in the car with them. Not wanting to leave my bike on the street, they lead me to a motel with secure underground parking and a trusted owner. If anyone had told me two days before that I would be leaving my bike in the garage of a stranger in Tijuana and jumping in a car with Mexican police, I would have told them they were crazy. Yet here I was in a Mexican police car riding through the streets of Tijuana, looking for a woman I barely knew who was my life-line. I quickly established a rapport with the two handsome, young cops by telling them I was a nurse and that my dad had been a cop in New Jersey. It established a comfort level that made our seemingly impossible endeavor appear reasonable.

It was getting dark and the urge to call someone to come rescue me was becoming powerful. I managed to be distracted by the intensity of the ride, which every few minutes was interrupted by the occasional "police event;" frantic U-turns, sirens whooping, cars pulled over, and even sharing the backseat with perpetrators who were totally confused at finding themselves sitting next to a blond biker chick from San Francisco. One of them even tried to talk to me nicely and found himself on the nasty end of a quick hand to the head swung from the front seat. And then, of course, there was the inevitable taco break, on them! We even managed a quick trip to the border to see if we could spot Karen in the line back to the U.S. No luck there either.

By now I was thinking it was time to make a phone call to someone. The last thing I wanted to do was call Larry or Maida so as to not cause them a moment's worry. Fortunately, at lunch, Karen and I had exchanged phone numbers of people to call if there was an emergency. She gave me a girlfriend's phone number and I gave her Dennis Casey's number. About 7:30 p.m. the cops agreed that I would likely be spending the night in Tijuana and offered to help me get a room at the hotel where we had left my BMW. On the way, we stopped at a leather and jewelry shop for the cops to spend some time joking around with their friend, Jack, the owner. When they told Jack my story he offered me his telephone to call Dennis Casey. The phone service between the U.S. and Mexico was lousy. After many busy signals Jack came up with some clever way, through a friend in San Diego, to interrupt Casey with an emergency call. It seemed to work, except this time instead of a busy signal we got Casey's answering machine. All I could do was leave a message. "Hey Dennis, I'm all right but I've lost Karen. If you hear from her, tell her to call the Tijuana police to get the name of the hotel where I'll be staying." "Hotel Leon," the cops shouted. I repeated it to Casey and prayed they'd have a phone where he could call.

The Hotel Leon in Tijuana, Mexico is where "fleabag" got its name. A dark, desperate room with no windows except for one in the bathroom looking down on the underground garage. The hallways echoed non-stop with the noise and chatter of giggly local girls and U.S. military men or college boys in search of some "fun." It wasn't hard to realize this safe haven was at least partially a brothel.

It was 11 p.m. and morning couldn't come fast enough. At least I was safe and my bike was safe. Sleep would be nice but I wasn't counting on it. Not that I had a clue as to what I'd do in the morning. All I could think of was that I hoped Karen had the sense to call Dennis so he could get a message to me and, fingers crossed, that she was alright and not too concerned about me. I knew she had a good head on her shoulders and that kept me reassured. No doubt when we relived this adventure we'd both wish we had done a least one thing differently. I hoped both of us would quickly see the lighter side and get on with the rest of our trip.

While trying to drift off to sleep I thought about Anne Morrow Lindbergh's book, *Gift From the Sea*, in which she urged, "Patience, patience, patience, is what the sea teaches. Patience and faith. One should lie empty, open, choiceless as a beach waiting for a gift from the sea." Well, I wasn't at the beach exactly, but I did feel marooned – marooned, lonely, confused, and upset. What I needed was a lot of patience and faith.

The next morning, by some miracle, Dennis and I connected. I must have sounded frantic and scared because Dennis quickly reminded me that "adventure was what I was looking for and this is what it looked like." It was a major lesson learned and as a result I never let panic or fright seep in or derail me again.

The good news was that Karen had called Dennis to let him know she was in Rosarito. I said, "Oh my God, is she at the Rosarito Hotel?" Mind you this was spring break, when all the good hotels are fully booked. Dennis said, "No, she's in a dump across the street." I was thrilled just to know where she was. I got on the bike and went down this gorgeous stretch of highway, this beautiful section of road that ran alongside the Pacific Ocean. It was early on a Sunday morning and there was very little traffic. A good hour later, I spotted the Rosarito exit and my heart leapt with joy, but only momentarily; as soon as I left the freeway it became a dirt road – my first dirt road. Clearly, we were in Mexico. I was puttering along slowly, dodging chickens and kids, and struggling with the road and the bike. Controlling your bike at high speed is easy, at low speed you start to feel the weight and you start to feel the slippage break. How you handle the braking is different. I rode until I got to the end where you then had to go back onto the freeway and I still didn't see Karen. Now my heart sank. All I could think was, "Oh my God, I thought this was going to be easy."

Dennis had said, "The dump across the road from the Rosarito Hotel." I managed to swing my bike perpendicular to the road to try to figure out what to do next when I looked back and there was Karen running up the road with a cup of coffee in her hand. I exploded, "Man, am I glad to see you." Then it was like nothing had happened. We certainly traded our stories (I don't think hers were anywhere near as interesting as mine) and we proceeded with the trip.

We went down the West Coast but also scooted over inland (to the Sea of Cortez side of Baja) where we went through a flock of monarch butterflies destroying a couple hundred of those on our own. I came within inches of being wiped off the face of the earth when I took a blind bend and a car nearly clipped me. It was one of those automatic reactions that saved me.

The other hazard we encountered was how two women motorcyclists could quickly gather a crowd of young men eager to try out their Latin charm on us. Karen led the way and taught me the distraction/dodge/run method and how to leave them in a trail of dust.

Another great lesson came when Karen ran low on gas and needed to syphon some fuel from a generous RV owner. Poor Karen ended up burping petrol fumes for miles. At our next break, she pulled out a cigarette. I gave her a wide berth. Who knows; she could have exploded! Fortunately, that didn't happen. What I did learn that day was how people on the road help each other and that would become valuable knowledge in my future travels.

By the end of our Baja trip, we had lost track of the calendar and ended up coming back a day early which made Karen furious. The school teacher coming back a day early from spring break — that just wasn't her style. She didn't want to confess to anybody that we had lost track of the days.

We returned to San Francisco in a horrible rainstorm. It was blinding all the way from somewhere south of the San Jose Airport to the Candlestick Park exit. At the San Jose airport, we stopped for a break and I said to Karen, "Listen, you know how to get home. I know where I live. I don't want you being responsible for me. You just get yourself home safely. I will too." She agreed and off we went in different directions. Dennis had told me earlier that truckers could be very, very good for motorcyclists. If you give them a signal they'll let you draft behind them. I was exhausted and scared out of my mind, but I tried this out on a Sunkist Lemonade truck and he gave me the okay to draft behind him, which kept me drier and relatively safe. And it also gave me this huge yellow lemon to look at which was comforting. I then decided to peel off at Candlestick Park and not do the rest of the freeway because my studio was down in that area. I was very familiar with all the streets, stop signs, red lights. I knew them all. Even though it was a dangerous neighborhood and it was probably around five o'clock in the evening. Even in a pouring rain, it's easier if you do it at slower speed so you are not blasted by water. I basically limped my way back to Presidio Terrace. Nobody was home. I picked up the phone, called Larry, and said, "I'm back." "Oh yeah, great. Let me pack up here in the office and I'll swing by and pick up some pizza," he said. A few minutes later, I got a phone call from him saying, "You're not going to believe this but I've been in a car accident. It was a minimal fender bender thing. I hate to tell you this, but I think the pizza will be cold." He came home and talked about the experience of having had this accident and never asked me a thing about my trip.

In June of that year, Maida graduated from high school. I had both my parents and Larry's parents come out for the graduation. One day we sat around in my kitchen and I told the whole story of the Mexico trip in front of everybody. I got on my soapbox and held court for probably thirty minutes retelling each and every crazy incident and "near miss." Their eyes bugged out. Looking back on it, I know it probably wasn't the kindest or most mature thing to do. But it felt right at the time and it was an interesting dynamic because both my parents and in-laws were there. So as much as my parents might have wanted to say, "What the hell were you doing?" and my in-laws would have loved to make a similar comment, none of them dared do it in front of one another. It was the first time Larry heard the story. As expected, he said nothing. They were all in shock. For me, it was a totally liberating experience.

CHAPTER 14

Travel Bug

1989

Most of our travel experiences as the Stupski family had been the predictable vacations that were put together by the Schwab Travel Department. Often we ended up going to the big Island of Hawaii where we stayed at the Schwab villa in the Mauna Kea Beach Hotel. Invariably we would show up at the front desk and Larry would be handed boxes of work sent by the company in advance of our arrival. I was getting tired of going on vacations where he would get on the plane with a stack of work and speed-read documents throughout the entire flight. This would be followed by a ritual of ripping everything up in a slow rhythmic way that made me want to take a gun to my head. I pitied the poor fellow passengers who sat near him.

On our last trip to Hawaii, when we arrived at the check-in desk and they started to haul out all the boxes the company had sent, I put my foot down and said, "Send them back to San Francisco." Fortunately, the hotel clerk listened to me. Larry wasn't grateful for my intervention. He loved his work and bringing it with him meant not having to deal with me and Maida. It was not a particularly pleasant vacation for any of us. The more time Larry and I had to spend together the clearer it became that he would rather be elsewhere.

I was still trying to find the magic that would turn things around in our marriage and from time to time I would invite another couple over for dinner in the hopes that spending time with people other than the Schwab folks would be good for Larry. One night I invited the president of the Art Institute and his wife over for dinner. Larry had met them previously and they all seemed to get along well. But at dinner, Larry sat at the head of the table, propped up like a king and was either unresponsive or sharp and snarky to anything that was said. It was impossible to get any kind of conversation going. The whole evening was an embarrassment. After they left, I confronted him and said, "What the hell is going on here? Why were you so distant and unfriendly and uncooperative when these lovely people were here?" His lack of response prompted me further. "You and I have to make some changes. Otherwise, I have no idea what's going to happen." Finally, he gave his curt answer. "As far as I'm concerned, you're the one in charge of the emotional well-being of this family and you're the one who needs to 'jump start it.'" In the blink of an eye, I saw clearly that for Larry it was pretty much over. I made a silent promise to myself, "That's it. Maida's going off to college and I'm going to be someplace else."

It was difficult to accept there was no saving our marriage. I had tried so hard for so long, but now both Larry and I knew it was just a matter of time before we split. Larry didn't want to be the "bad guy" and ask for a divorce, so the ball was in my court. The details of our finances remained a mystery to me, but I imagined that Larry was probably loathe to split fifty-fifty whatever assets we had. For me, the money wasn't the primary issue. I just wanted enough to live on and I wanted out.

I was thinking hard about what direction my life would take when Dennis Casey came up with an interesting idea about running motorcycle tours out of Las Vegas for Japanese tourists. His plan was to fly them in for long weekends, provide them with a small, rather inexpensive style Harley, and take them out on a tour. In Dennis's research, he learned there are no deserts in Japan and that citizens are not allowed to have guns. He figured this would be a chance for these tourists to experience the open road and go to a rifle range where they could experience the "Wild Wild West" as part of their great motorcycle adventure.

I thought that sounded like a reasonable idea. I had a little money set aside and I decided to use some of it to finance this new venture. The first thing Dennis and I did was buy a prototype motorcycle for what we imagined would eventually become a fleet of bikes. We thought the perfect bike would be a low to the ground, easy to handle Harley. It had to be a Harley because that was the "Easy Rider" image that all foreigners had of American motorcyclists. Dennis flew to the Harley-Davidson factory in Milwaukee, picked up the bike and rode it back to San Francisco.

Neither of us had ever run a bike tour, but we knew the bike world and we knew there were certain things you could do to get good advertising and build a customer base. It didn't seem to be that difficult. We were truly excited about our venture and I was happy to have something to look forward to. Then Dennis did something that would drastically change both our lives.

Dennis loved to go off on all kinds of excursions and one day he decided that he and a buddy would go to Australia for a couple of weeks. They went "down under," bought a jalopy to tour around in, did some bicycling, and came home gorgeous and tanned. He walked into my studio looking like a million bucks, thrilled with everything that had happened on his amazing Australia trip. He couldn't stop talking about it.

I, on the other hand, was under a cloud, moping around because Maida was in her last year of high school and the time was approaching when she would start college, and Larry and I would be left alone. Without our daughter as a buffer, it felt like things would rapidly go from bad to worse. Dennis read my mind. He said, "I think once Maida's off to college you should just blow out of town for a while. Take a trip — kind of restart the clock. Maybe take a trip to Australia!"

Sometimes the answer you're searching so hard for has been waiting under your nose the whole time. For almost a year I had been looking at a scrap of newspaper that had been given to me by the seventeen-year-old neighbor boy I used to ride with. It was an advertisement for a book that listed all the motorcycle touring companies in the world. That piece of newspaper sat in my inbox for months. It would come up and I would push it down; then it would come up again and I would push it down. But once Dennis put the bug in my ear, I dug up that newspaper clipping and ordered the book. Fortunately, it contained an amazing compilation of worldwide motorcycle tours. I went straight to the chapter on Australia and began dreaming about my next adventure.

There were three or four Australian companies that claimed to run motorcycle tours. They all sounded pretty much the same. You show up, they provide a bike and whatever else you need, and off you'd go on an adventure with the tour guide. The one listing that struck me was the Australian Motorcycle Touring Company, run by a fellow named Geoff Coat, who had BMW motorcycles. Part of the attraction (besides having the right bikes) was that the company worked with a travel agency in Berkeley. That meant I didn't have to deal with the time change and figure out how to get in touch with somebody in Australia. I was able to go over to Berkeley and talk to the agency person about what the trip entailed, like getting my own plane ticket and whether I would be bringing my own helmet or not. After satisfying all my questions, they let me know that if I was seriously interested, I could put a deposit down on a trip and let them know when I was ready to go.

Part of my rationale for going to Australia was that I would be doing first-hand research on how to run a motorcycle tour for the benefit of Dennis' and my new enterprise. I knew nothing about the owner Geoff Coat, other than he had been included in the reference guide, but I went with my gut instinct and plunked down my deposit for a trip that would leave the following October after Maida was off to college.

On an early July evening I was feeling particularly lighthearted, having just enjoyed seeing the film, *When Harry Met Sally*. I returned home to find my phone machine flashing insistently. I picked it up and heard a grim message from my father, "Your sister had a bad fall and is in the hospital. All we know is that she may not be alive when you get here. Please come as fast as you can."

I dropped everything and left for North Carolina. My dad came to pick me up at the airport and I was relieved to see from his body language that my sister was still alive. The story of Karen's accident was sketchy. Mom had gone over to Karen's house in the morning because she and Karen had planned to defrost and clean Karen's big freezer. Mom was concerned because she hadn't received an expected call confirming their plan. She had left several messages but still hadn't heard from Karen. As she approached the front door the frenzied barking of my sister's dog alarmed my mother and when she opened the door, she found Karen lying unconscious at the bottom of the stairs with a basket of laundry strewn around her. Apparently, she had tripped or fallen over the dog and tumbled down headfirst, slamming into a wall at the bottom of the stairs. It was estimated that she had lain there for almost twelve hours. Her husband Marshall had been out of town and didn't learn of the accident until his return. My father, who never cared for Marshall, put his "cop" hat on and considered that, "without any evidence to the contrary, it was quite possible that Marshall had actually been there and pushed Karen down the stairs." No charges were ever brought, but Dad was never convinced of Marshall's innocence.

For the next three months, my weekends were spent flying back and forth to North Carolina. I spent as much time as I could with my sister, praying for a sign that she would wake up. My nursing skills were put to good use as I helped out with her care whenever I could. While the nursing staff was conscientious about bathing Karen, I became aware that her hair hadn't been washed since the accident. I knew exactly how to do it and convinced the nurse on duty to assist me. There was still some dried blood caked in Karen's hair and as I struggled to get a comb through it, she suddenly burst out with, "Ow, that hurts!" It was one of those great, hoped for moments — when the patient in a coma suddenly wakes up. We were overjoyed and hopeful. Her condition was still very serious, but this was definitely a positive sign. I breathed a deep sigh of relief. I knew that even if she continued to improve, she was facing many months of rehab, but she had made some meaningful progress and I felt I could go back to San Francisco.

IN SEPTEMBER 1989, it was time to get Maida to Occidental College where she would start her freshman year. Our car wasn't quite big enough for all the girl stuff she had to take so Larry rented a bigger car. I was assigned to the back seat and jealously watched the motorcyclists that went by, thinking how much more interesting it would be to be making the trip that way.

We arrived at Occidental College, got Maida settled into her dorm and Larry and I checked into a local Pasadena hotel. We dutifully took part in the school's "introduction to parents" and the "welcome freshmen" ceremonies. On our final night we hugged Maida, wished her well and gave her all those last-minute instructions you give the child you are about to separate from, ending with the final advice, "If you need anything just pick up the phone." The words sounded hollow and clichéd because in fact there are no right words for that painful moment when you leave your only child in unfamiliar surroundings to begin a life completely apart from your own. Larry and I rode back to our hotel in silence, each pondering the enormous changes we both knew were coming.

The next morning when I got up, Larry was already in the shower. That wasn't unusual; he was always an early riser, but when he came out of the bathroom fully dressed in a suit and tie, I was surprised. "We're driving back to the Bay Area." I said, "What's the deal with the suit?" He said, "I decided last minute. I'm just going to take a plane back. I've got a meeting I need to go to." That meant I would be driving the rental car back on my own. I stood there a moment while the tumblers in my brain clicked into place. I looked up at him and said, "Okay, and by the time you come home, I will have moved out." He shed a tear, picked up his briefcase and left.

⌒

ON THE TOP FLOOR OF THE Presidio Terrace house, Larry and I had created a wonderful new bedroom with a walk-in closet that was big enough for both of us. Now, not even the most spacious home in San Francisco was big enough for both of us. The next day I arranged to have every single stitch of my clothing removed from that beautiful closet and shipped to my Bayview studio.

I walked away from Presidio Terrace the same way I had walked away from every previous house we owned, without ever looking back.

I went from living in the lap of luxury to the bleak narrow confines of what had once been a place of temporary refuge. Neither Larry nor I said anything to Maida about our separation. We didn't want to inflict that pain on her while she was still in the process of finding her way at Occidental. While Larry and I may no longer have loved each other, we both still loved our daughter.

We told very few people what was going on and the pretense of carrying on a "normal" life began weighing heavily on me. I continued to fly to Charlotte weekly where I still had to pick up the pieces of Karen's recovery. There were constant new care problems, often created by my brother-in-law and the medical staff. My other duty was to handhold my parents through the most traumatic event of their lives. Eventually, we received the good news that my sister would survive her severe head injury. We had yet to know what the lingering effects of that fall might be; if she would ever regain her memory and her physical mobility, but at least she would live. She was in rehab and her husband was now fully in charge. Luckily this all resolved before I was scheduled to leave.

Ten days later I was on a plane to Melbourne, Australia.

Margo, Dod and me at Capistrano,
California, 1945

Dod's Graduation from the
New Jersey State Police Academy, 1950

The Laguna Beach Police Chief, his wife, Mrs. Bocker,
and me, Laguna Beach, California, 1946

A proud St. Michael's High School
twirler, 1960

My graduation as a
Registered Nurse, 1965

Engagement Photo, 1966

Wedding to Larry Stupski, January
28, 1967, Elkton Maryland

One of my proudest days. Receiving my Bachelor of Fine Arts degree
from the San Francisco Art Institute, 1983

Maida and me at Occidental College, 1989

CHAPTER 15

Down Under Wonder

October-November 1989

In October of 1989, as I was flying into Melbourne's Tullamarine Airport, I had two distinct thoughts: "I didn't expect Mediterranean-style tiled roofs!" and "I think I've been here before!" After winding my way through airport customs, I was relieved to see a sign held high with my name printed boldly on it. The man holding the sign was the owner of the Australian Motorcycle Touring Company, Geoff Coat. My first impression of him was that he looked like my mother's side of the family, especially Uncle Francie -- ruddy, Irish maybe? Instantly I felt a reassuring family connection and a sense that Australia was a place I was going to be very comfortable exploring.

Geoff was very jovial. He had a gorgeous smile and laughed right away at the fact that I didn't know which side of the car to get into – it was the left. We chatted all way to the hotel and he dropped me off with the arrangement to have dinner that night with the other passenger on our tour. We were a group of only two, me and a young man from the British Army who was on leave. I was hoping to join a convivial group, but since there was nothing I could do about it, I decided to make the best of it.

Once in my room, I decided to call Larry, ostensibly to tell him I'd arrived safely in Australia; in truth I was still hoping to rekindle things. I was looking at the crumbling of a twenty-three-year marriage. I thought maybe Larry and I could have a new kind of adventure together. I suggested that he could meet me in Sydney after the ten-day motorcycle part was over. I was pipe-dreaming. Larry wasn't the least bit interested.

Dinner that night with Geoff and the other tour guest was pleasant and we seemed like a compatible threesome. Geoff gave us a brief introduction to our itinerary, which would cover almost two thousand miles, and told me about the bike he had picked out for me. It was a bit bigger than I was used to. Instead of 650 ccs, it was 800 ccs. But I was sure I could handle it. The next morning when we all met at the Peter Meneres BMW car and bike dealership, where Geoff operated from, I discovered the bike was taller and a bit more tippy-toe for me than I was used to. Plus, when I had to do a U-turn it was in the opposite direction which practically made me lose my breakfast on the spot. (Driving is on the left – British style.) Geoff was patient and helped me survive it and once we were on the open road I felt a lot more comfortable. The Mulga Tour, named for a tree that grew throughout this particular region, offered a variety of superb scenery; much of it looked just like California. Every day brought new surprises. We rode into the "gold country," which was similar to our American West, then into the agricultural fruit belt and along the lush Yarra River, lined with willows and gray-green eucalyptus style trees. Along the way we saw orchards and wetlands and hundreds of birds including exotic Egyptian Ibis. The following day, we left the rolling hillsides and went from orchard country to a warmer climate where grapes for raisins were grown. (Raisins are called sultanas in Australia, so I learned not to ask for Raisin Bran, because all they have is Sultana Bran.)

The Yarra River, while not very wide, is a major waterway which separates New South Wales and Victoria. At that time, New South Wales was one of the few places in Australia where gambling casinos were legal. That night we stayed right on the border of New South Wales and Victoria in a lovely brick hotel with a long, graceful lawn and I indulged in a little gambling. Geoff had established warm friendships with all the families who owned the hotels and motels along the way and wherever we went it was like a reunion. Much to my surprise it was traditional to have our breakfast served in our rooms – often through a slot in the wall.

The next day, we were on the road less than ten minutes when the scenery changed drastically. Suddenly, we were in the Outback where hardly anything grew. It took on a desert like fragrance with colors quite unlike anything I had seen. Most notably, we began seeing caution signs with silhouettes of kangaroos or emus. They were a real danger, much like deer crossing the road. They could appear out of nowhere. It took me quite a while to spot them, because they're the same color as the ground. If by chance we would spot one, Geoff would cautiously pull us over to take our cameras out and see if we could get a photo. Most of the time the kangaroos or emus didn't hang around for very long.

Another distinct change was the characteristics of the petrol stations, which were very basic, often with diesel engines going on in the background. Pretty much any car that would be passing by would pull in to fill up. You just never wanted to take a chance because the distances between petrol stations were so extreme. Every day of the journey was completely different from the previous day making the entire tour seem like one magnificent scroll unrolling before our eyes.

The other great benefit of the tour was that along the way I gained a whole new level of riding skills. Geoff had ridden his first motorbike at the age of nine and everything came so naturally to him that sometimes he found it hard to explain what he was doing or why he did it. But he was very patient with me because he understood that I came late to the motorcycle game, and I didn't have the sort of natural reflexes that a kid would have. I had to learn everything the hard way. I bombarded Geoff with questions and closely observed his technique as I rode along behind him. I came up against some heart pounding situations, like how to deal with the dynamics of going around a bend. Geoff carefully explained how the bike had these opposing cylinders which caused a gyration that you had to fight. The bike wanted to stay straight but you could override that with the slightest change of the handlebars. As he described the gyroscopic aspect of this particular machine, I became aware that he was giving me much more than what I had signed up for.

Geoff was a smoker and we would make these occasional smoke stops at interesting places which gave us a chance to take in the scenery. Sometimes there was a structure for some shade or sometimes you might find a source of water. On our first day out, we pulled over at one stop where there was a car that was stalled and needed a crank to get it started. Geoff had trained as a mechanical engineer in the Australian army, and he volunteered to help out. I was impressed by the generosity of his spirit and as he leaned over to crank the engine he turned and gave me this big grin. I thought, "Wow, this guy is kind of cute."

By the second day on the road, it was obvious to both of us that we were connecting on a personal level and within days we became intimately involved in what could best be described as a "shipboard romance." On the next to the last day of the tour, we made plans to have dinner and spend the night together. Geoff was a sensitive, caring lover and in the morning, I awoke more relaxed and happy than I had felt in years. All I could think of was, "Oh, my God, this guy is so special." The thrill of the motorcycle tour was enhanced ten-fold by our love affair. Our British soldier pal must have felt like the odd-man-out, but he hung in there enjoying the trip as best he could. By the end of the ten-day tour, I had seen enough of Australia to know that I could grow to love it and I had seen enough of Geoff Coat to know that I didn't want this to ever end.

The final day of the tour had us finishing where we started at Peter Meneres BMW where I went to drop off my bike and collect any personal gear I had left for safe keeping. A friendly guy in the office offered me a ride back to my hotel. As we drove, he asked where I was from. When I said San Francisco, he looked at me solemnly,

"Mate, do I have news for you!"

My heart stopped!

"They had an earthquake. A big one. Magnitude 6.9. About sixty people dead. Bridges and freeways all torn up."

By the time I got to my hotel room, the blood was pounding in my head and I was barely holding back my panic. All phone lines were down in San Francisco, but fortunately I was able to get in touch with Maida who was in Los Angeles at Occidental College. She had managed to get through to Larry before the phones went dead and he assured her that everything in the house was fine including the cats and the dog. A couple of wine glasses had broken, but that was it. I breathed a big sigh of relief. Once I knew Maida was fine, Larry was fine and the dog and the two cats were fine, I stood there thinking, "Okay, now what?" Obviously, there was nothing else I could do so I stuck to my schedule. I took off the next day and flew to Sydney.

⁓

IN SYDNEY, I HAD BOOKED a room in a lovely hotel where they served high tea with fine china and crystal, and a classical piano player performed live every afternoon in the posh foyer. Despite my concerns about the earthquake, I decided to enjoy myself; "I'm here, I might as well do the touristy thing." I wandered around the city taking in all the charming sites, the street performers, the Sydney Opera House and the waterfront where I ran into two young American girls proudly wearing, "I survived the San Francisco earthquake!" T-shirts; all of it with one thought in mind, "This would be much more fun if Geoff was with me."

Every night, Geoff and I were on the phone with each other. In those calls, I got to know a lot more about his life. I was already aware that he was married but that he and his wife had been on the outs for a while, just like Larry and me. They had two adopted sons; one was already out of the house and they were just waiting for the other son to go off on his own. I knew my arrival might speed up their separation, which I was not proud of, but undeniable circumstances had thrust us together. I was hungry for love and so was Geoff. Everything about him was what my heart had been aching for, including the fact that he had been in the military, which greatly increased his attraction in my eyes. He was the embodiment of the precious icons of my childhood – my U.S. Marine Corps and New Jersey State Trooper dad, and that treasured plastic toy of a uniformed man on a motorcycle. And now here he was, the manifestation of all that had been precious to me as a little girl. How could I possibly say no to that?

On my last night in Sydney, we glumly said our phone goodbyes. I packed my bags and prepared to fly home. The next morning, I discovered that fate had one last twist in store for me. I awoke to the news that all flights to and from San Francisco had been cancelled due to massive damage from the earthquake. I took my cue and caught the first flight back to Melbourne.

Geoff was booked to run a three-day weekend tour (developed for locals) for an Australian girl with her American biker boyfriend. It turned out to be the perfect romantic weekend for all four of us. That short trip put an end to any doubts about the deep feelings Geoff and I had for each other. By the end of the trip, we knew we were in an exciting "full of possibilities" relationship. The following day the San Francisco airport reopened, and I flew home. The minute I got on the plane I started planning my return trip to Australia.

BEFORE I WENT TO AUSTRALIA, Dennis and I had taken a brief exploratory motorcycle trip to Las Vegas to scope out an itinerary for our touring company. By the time I finished the Mulga Tour, I had already decided to dump the U.S. touring business. When I met with Dennis and told him I wasn't going to pursue Las Vegas, he was furious with me in a way that forever changed our relationship. The truth was, after my experience with Geoff, I was no longer personally invested in starting up a touring company the way Dennis was. He was looking for a way to make a living that didn't include doing construction work. But for me, I was in love. I was in lust. I was head-over-heels. My brain was endlessly spinning on how I could create a bi-hemispheric life that would involve spending a great deal of my time in Australia. My interest in starting a new business in America was definitely at an all-time low. There wasn't anything I wanted more than to be in Australia with Geoff Coat, the man I had fallen madly in love with.

I knew I had to be straight with Dennis. When I finally told him I was pulling out of the Las Vegas tour business, he was so furious he picked up the first thing he could find and threw it at me. He was both mad and disappointed. I really couldn't blame him, and I probably shouldn't have been surprised by his reaction. Dennis was a recovering alcoholic and often had what I call "dry drunks." Once he had vented his anger, he went dark on me. There was no contact, no phone calls. I felt terrible. We had been close friends for many years, and he had seen me through a lot of difficult times. I wanted it to go differently, but I had to make a decision. My heart wasn't in a start-up Las Vegas motorcycle tour business – my heart was in Australia.

IN AN EFFORT TO MAINTAIN some kind of family tradition for Maida, I decided to make a home cooked Thanksgiving dinner at the Presidio Terrace family home. In my usual "all-out" style I did the whole thing – turkey, stuffing, cranberry sauce – all the while imagining that while we enjoyed a holiday meal together, Larry and I could catch up on how Maida was doing in college. I was in a good place emotionally and I thought everyone else would be too. Unfortunately, that was not the case. The issues that had caused us to separate were still bubbling under the surface. Things went from bad to worse and finally got to the point where I walked out. I left Maida and Larry there with my beautiful dinner and retreated to the tiny room I was renting.

I knew that Christmas would prove to be equally painful. It was becoming harder and harder to find a reason not to go straight back to Australia. I looked at the calendar and knew Geoff had another eight-day Boomerang Tour going out at the beginning of January. That was all the excuse I needed. I left San Francisco on Christmas Eve. By the time I arrived in Melbourne, I had lost Christmas on the International Dateline. I landed in Melbourne on Boxing Day, December 26, 1990. Again, Geoff was there to greet me at the airport, looking even better than I remembered. Again, we couldn't keep our hands off each other. We headed straight for a romantic afternoon at the four-star Regent Hotel, which we spent high up on the

44th floor overlooking the incredible expanse of Melbourne. I had brought Geoff some Christmas gifts, including a watch I had special ordered from a *Sky Mall* magazine – you provide the image and they make the watch face. I had chosen the logo of Geoff's company, Australian Motorcycle Touring, for his watch face. He loved it. It made me happy just to see him so happy. In return, Geoff gave me a small green bag issued by the Australian Army when he was in Vietnam and a military brooch used to create their infamous "slouch hats." Before the day was over, we were talking about our future, including the possibility of finding me an art studio in Melbourne. We were on the same wavelength about everything. All I could think of was, "I've got to be the luckiest woman in the world."

BESIDES RUNNING HIS MOTORCYCLE tours, Geoff was also employed by Daimler Benz and had to keep up with a busy work schedule. In addition, he was president of the BMW Motorcycle Club which held an annual Christmas Camp in the city of Thoona, about three hours north of Melbourne. Due to a work-related trip, Geoff was unable to attend but he made arrangements for me to attend notifying several of his friends to be on the lookout for my arrival. Our relationship was still a secret among his friends and I was presented as Geoff's American client who wanted to get in some additional biking experience in Australia.

It was a couple of days before the Christmas Camp would start and I took the opportunity to pay a surprise visit to a former Schwab employee, Rich Arnold, who along with his wife, Vivien, had moved to a horse ranch in the town of Echuca, not too far from Thoona where the Christmas Camp would take place. It was great to have American friends who were already established residents of Australia. I showed up at their door completely unexpected, but they welcomed me in like a long-lost friend. It was a fun packed visit and a great way to start my trip.

The next day I set off to the BMW Christmas Camp where I was warmly greeted by a generous and amusing group of motorcyclists who instantly accepted me as one of their own. As I rolled out my sleeping bag by the campfire, I wished that I could let everyone know the real reason I was there. Some of them appeared to notice that the bag I was sleeping in belonged to Geoff. I wondered how long it would be before people began putting two and two together.

In the morning, various side trips were arranged for the riders. I joined one going to nearby Yarrawonga, a small town situated on the south bank of Australia's longest waterway, the Murray River. It was another beautiful ride, but around 1 p.m. I was already itching to be back in Geoff's arms. I knew he would be back from his business trip so I took off on my own and headed to Melbourne where Geoff had arranged a motel room for me. By the time I navigated through the Melbourne traffic and checked in, I was pretty exhausted. I wearily made my way to the room, slipped my key in the lock, and opened the door to find a bouquet of flowers and four love notes from Geoff – just the lift a really tired biker needed. Again, I asked myself, "How did I come to have this truly unbelievable man in my life?"

CHAPTER 16

Nullarbor Challenge

1989-1990

The next morning, Saturday, December 30th, Geoff was scheduled to lead another three-day Great Escape Weekend Tour. Ann, a writer for a London- based publication, was coming along to do a story on Geoff's touring company. She wasn't a biker but would be riding as a passenger on the back of Geoff's bike. It was important that the ride went well. If Ann's article was complimentary, it could mean a lot for Geoff's business. At 8 a.m. the next morning, we met up at the BMW dealership with Ann and our other rider, Joe, a Californian who worked for Merrill-Lynch. Joe and Ann had no idea that Geoff and I were romantically involved. As far as they knew, I was just another client on the tour.

Our first destination was Mansfield, a small-town set in the green rolling foothills of the Victorian Alps about 110 miles northeast of Melbourne. We arrived in time to enjoy a visit to the Healeseville Sanctuary Wildlife Refuge and then checked in for our overnight stay. Geoff and I were on our best behavior until we were certain that Ann and Joe were both safely tucked away for the night. Then I tiptoed over to his room where we shared another magical night together.

The next day we headed south on a beautiful three-and-a-half-hour ride through long, warm, honey-colored valleys dotted with prickly native trees. Our destination was Phillip Island, a favorite tourist spot where motorcyclists often congregated and were welcomed. We all enjoyed an afternoon at the motorcycle races and a New Year's Eve dinner together. Ann and Joe were humorous and intelligent companions and our little group of four had quickly grown close. It was getting harder to keep our secret from them. By that evening, Geoff and I no longer cared what anyone thought about us. It was New Year's Eve and we wanted to be together. Geoff sat Ann down for a long talk and explained our situation. It was a bit tricky because when Geoff invited Ann on the tour, he offered her the guesthouse at his family home to spend the night before flying back home. Now Ann would have to meet Geoff's wife, Maxine, with the uncomfortable knowledge of our secret. Ann took it all in, noting that it might be a bit sticky, but she responded in the best way possible – she was very pleased for us. That night I shared Geoff's Phillips Island cottage to celebrate the most memorable New Year's Eve I've ever had. I was filled with a joy beyond belief and wished it was a harbinger of happiness for the new decade.

The next day on our way back to Melbourne, we stopped for lunch and let Joe in on our secret. He may already have guessed the truth, but he never let on. Like Ann, he too expressed happiness for us. It was liberating to share our joy with our two new friends.

In Melbourne, Geoff packed Ann off to stay with Maxine for the night while I waited for him to join me in the nearby suburban shopping center of Glen Waverley. Things must have gone badly with Maxine, because when he returned he was very upset. At my behest, he had given up smoking but now he broke his resolution by having a couple of cigarettes. To his credit once he calmed down he threw the rest of the pack away. That night I further soothed him by giving him a full body massage – the first one he ever had – oh how he loved it! And so did I. I'd never been with a man who was so grateful for all I had to give. Happy, happy me!

The rest of the week was spent preparing for the upcoming Boomerang Tour. This time Geoff and I would be the only ones on the tour and we would be openly traveling as a couple. Geoff was scouting for new destinations on upcoming tours. Some places Geoff already had relationships with. Others weren't aware that our presence might bring them additional business. The eight-day tour took us north through the vast range of scenery from Mount Buffalo National Park, with its sheer rock granite cliffs up to Khancoban, a small mountain town in New South Wales near Australia's highest peak, Mount Kosciuszko. We spent a day in Canberra, Australia's capital city, before heading down to the farming community of Braidwood. The trip down from Canberra's 1,900-foot elevation to Braidwood, at sea level, was made in a terrifying pea-soup fog. My heart was in my mouth the whole time, but following Geoff's lead kept me focused and steady on my motorcycle. My admiration for his biking skills grew daily and as he led me through every kind of terrain and weather condition, I became confident in my own skills as well. The sixth day of the trip was spent in the beautiful Lakes Entrance, a seaside playground in eastern Victoria. Our final destination took us back to Victoria, to a place I was already familiar with, Phillip Island. Geoff and I had been there not more than ten days before on our Weekend Escape Tour. When we returned as a couple, Peter, the owner, and his wife didn't quite know what to make of it. This was a place Geoff had been to many times, often with his wife Maxine. In fact, Maxine and her mother had just left after spending a few days there. Explanations were made and I could see this was just the beginning of a difficult transition period for Geoff. He was going to have to let all his friends know and it was possible that some of them would not take it well. Fortunately, Gary and Nick, Geoff's mates at Meneres BMW, had come around to accepting me – it was a start.

At the end of the eight-day Boomerang Tour, Geoff and I were more infatuated and more committed to each other than ever. Whatever difficulties might lie ahead, we were ready to face them. On our last day, we took an early morning walk on the beach. It was completely deserted and seemingly existed for us alone. We had a camera with a timer on it and had great fun snapping silly photos of ourselves. Geoff found a pair of flip-flops that had washed up on the shore and presented them to me as a gift, which I treasured. It was a day filled with joy and tinged with sadness. Our time alone was about to be over. Geoff would be leaving Melbourne for two weeks on business and I would basically be left on my own. On the spur of the moment, I decided that rather than wait around moping, I would continue my motorcycle adventure by taking a trip to visit a friend in Perth.

～

PHILOMENA ROURKE WAS an Australian woman I met in Goddess Camp the previous summer. She was married, had kids, and had come to America on her own adventure, which included attending Goddess Camp. We enjoyed each other's company and stayed in contact. When I was considering an Australia motorcycle trip, I asked her what she thought about it. She was all for it, "You'll love Australia, you'll be fine. And when you come down, you must visit me in Perth." At the time, that option seemed out of the question. I said, "Philomena, that's probably not going to happen. I don't even know where Melbourne and Sydney are, let alone Perth. Plus, if I do come to Australia, it will only be for a short time – I'll do my eight-day motorcycle tour, check out Sydney and go right back to the States."

Now, so many things had changed that the idea of visiting Philomena in Perth seemed perfectly logical. Geoff was not happy about it; he thought it was too dangerous for somebody who was new to motorcycling and that I didn't know what I'd be getting myself into. I was feeling very confident of my riding skills and said, "Fine, if you won't give me a bike, I'll find somebody else who will." It was the first taste Geoff had of my willfulness and he must have respected it because he said, "Okay, at least I know my bike will keep you safe and you won't have any mechanical problems." Admittedly, I questioned my decision once or twice about crossing unknown terrain, but the drive to challenge myself was greater than any fears I had. Looking back on the insecure, hesitant, convention bound young woman I once was, to the independent, daring, biker I had become, I knew that no matter what difficulties I would face, the rewards would be worth the challenge. Geoff gave me a bike and his blessing and on Friday, January 12th at 8:30 a.m. I took off on my solo trip across Australia.

My first day out, from Melbourne to Adelaide was uneventful, other than being stopped by a cop for speeding outside the town of Horsham. Fortunately, the officer was more interested in my story than in giving me a ticket and he let me go with a warning to "slow down whenever you're entering a town." I promised I would follow his advice and that was that. The weather was good and I arrived in the capital city at around 7 p.m.; time enough to have a great phone talk with Geoff and to let him know that my first day was a breeze.

The next day I headed due north through the familiar Adelaide Hills wine country to reach the Flinders Ranges National Park. I arrived at the Pichi Richi Pass where I had been before on a previous trip with Geoff. From that point on, I was venturing into unfamiliar terrain. At the top of the ridge, I took a left and was suddenly smacked in the face with the enormity of my crazy adventure. At that 1500-foot elevation I got my first glimpse of what lay before me – the biggest expanse of desert I had ever encountered. My heart dropped so fast it literally went "boom." All I could think was, "Man – what have I gotten myself into?" No wonder Geoff had been concerned for my safety. But now, I had something to prove and there was no turning back.

In truth, I had been testing myself for the past ten years – taking baby steps, inching my way along. Everything from art school to getting my motorcycle license had been attempts to prove that I was in fact the courageous, daring Linda Dodwell I felt myself to be and not the mere shadow of a Linda who had been boxed in, limited, ignored and ridiculed into compliance.

As I surveyed what lay before me – my heart pounding like mad – the real Linda stood up and said, "I can do this." I let out my clutch, twisted my throttle and roared ahead.

At Port Augusta, I took a left and headed down the Peninsula toward the town of Whyalla, which I later learned means "windy" in Aborigine. Whyalla definitely lived up to its name. A stiff wind fought me all the way into town. If the trip down the Peninsula was going to be anything like this, the scenery wasn't going to be worth the struggle. I was hoping to find someone to advise me, but the town appeared to be empty. Even the large BP (British Petroleum) facility which normally would be bustling with activity stood silent. Finally, I realized it was Saturday. That meant almost everything was closed. I couldn't find a single person and I was in desperate need of some local input. That's when I saw the petrol station – always a welcome sight. This one even had a milk bar – a convenience store where you could get coffee and snacks. By now the heat had become intense and I was craving an ice cream bar – what they call a paddle pop. A friendly couple ran the milk bar and were obviously surprised and intrigued by my sudden appearance. They looked me up and down before asking, "Well, where are you going?" I told them about Perth and Philomena and I asked what I should expect on the Peninsula. They shot a quick look at each other and then at me and said, "You know what? We think you should turn around and get back on that road. Don't have anything to do with the Peninsula." Obviously, the Peninsula was not the scenic route I had imagined and they cautioned me away from what might have been a treacherous journey. "You get back on that road until you come to an intersection at a place called Iron Knob. Take a left and just keep going." I paid for my paddle pop and thanked them for the information.

My destination was the town of Wudinna, where I would spend the night. I figured I could probably make it there around 4:00 or 4:30, which was always my goal—to get in before the kangaroos came out. Being nocturnal creatures, they show up at dusk and are extremely hard to distinguish from the surrounding desert. I knew from my travels with Geoff how dangerous the "roos" could be and that it was best to be safely tucked inside your digs before night fell. The remainder of the trip included intense heat, threatening storm clouds, incredible loneliness, and growing fatigue. Fortunately, with my newfound mental resolve, I was energized for the rigors of the journey. When I finally reached Wudinna, I was thankful I had made it there safely and the modest lodging the town had to offer, the Wudinna Motel, seemed a cozy haven.

As I had learned on my Baja trip, all I really needed was a lock on my door, clean sheets, and hot water. The Wudinna Motel met all my requirements and my grateful body collapsed on the bed for a much-needed rest. As I closed my eyes my body still hummed from the bruising vibration of the bike. When you're on a motorcycle, all your senses are engaged: you

feel the heat, you feel the cold, you feel the insects, you smell the vegetation as you pass by, you smell the individual scent of every variety of
eucalyptus tree, you smell a fire burning in the distance and you smell the
scent of the not always visible roadkill. Your entire sensory mechanism is
bombarded. No wonder I was so exhausted.

As I lay in bed waiting for sleep to overtake me, I re-evaluated my
undertaking. It was far greater than I had imagined. This was going to be
a test, not only of my stamina, but of my fortitude, to complete such a
journey.

CHAPTER 17

Surprise in Perth

January 1990

The next day I arose refreshed and ready to do it all again. No doubt the sweet and loving wake-up call from Geoff helped. While checking out of the Wudinna Motel, I spotted a bulletin board filled with messages from people trying to locate each other by carrying on conversations back and forth in notes scrawled on scraps of paper. Some of them were filled with concern about a missing loved one while others were more lighthearted; "Hey George, meet up at the motel bar at 6:00." It was something I would see repeatedly at motels and rest stops along the way and it made me feel I was part of some larger community of solitary travelers who all had the same need to connect with other sojourners.

It was the little breaks along the way that kept me sane. In Ceduna, I had to stop at a border control checkpoint and like most right side of the road drivers of the world I pulled up to the wrong side of the booth. When I came up on the wrong side the border guard said, "So where are you from in the US?" I caught it right away and said, "Oh my God, I'm so sorry." He, like so many people along the way, was quite amazed that I was doing this solo trip and was very encouraging, assuring me that I would be just fine. He even wrote down the border patrol phone number in case of emergency. I was grateful to those I would later refer to as "my travel angels": the couple in a petrol station in Whyalla, then later an elderly caravan member.

Folks would pop up at just the right time with an answer to a question I didn't even know to ask.

Later that day I stopped for gas and encountered a group of "Gray Nomads," retirees who drive caravans (we call them trailers or RV's) and travel together in a long line to explore their own country. Sure enough, as soon as I pulled in, a kindly gentleman with a mischievous twinkle in his eye was delegated to come over and "chat me up" to find out what I was up to. After I told him my story, he leaned in confidentially and said, "Somewhat down the road, you're going to see a brown sign with a camera drawn on it. I want you to pay attention and take a left there. It will be well worth your while." I wanted to press him for more details, but he held up his hand, shook his head and would say no more. I nodded, "Okay, thanks," and took off. It was a good stretch down the road before I finally saw the innocuous 10" x 12" inch sign. As instructed, I turned down the dirt path. Within eyesight of the highway, I encountered a large rusting piece of construction equipment with a plaque attached to it explaining that this machine had been used to pave the road. I thought to myself, "Well that's typical for a guy. He wants to show me this historic monument to road paving!"

Obviously, it was no big deal to me, but I recognized that it must have solved a big problem for those travelers who for decades had to cope with a badly rutted, dirt road. I could even see how challenging it must have been for the Gray Nomads, especially when it rained. So I gave the old gentleman his due and acknowledged that having this nice smooth road was something to be proud of. That's when I noticed a well-trodden foot path branching off to the right. I thought, "Well I'll just tootle on down there and see what everyone's curious about."

Nothing could have prepared me for what I saw next. I had crossed so much flat terrain over the past three days I had no notion I had been navigating for 720 miles, at 200 to 400 feet above sea level for hours…days. When I came to the end of the path and stepped into the clearing, I found myself on the edge of a cliff as high as any I'd ever stood upon, overlooking a breathtaking view of the Great Australian Bight, that sensual curve of the Indian Ocean that creates a spectacular shoreline all the way from

South Australia to Western Australia. It was startling and exciting. I looked around for someone to share the moment with, but there wasn't another living being anywhere in sight. It was just the sky, the ocean, these monumental cliffs, and me. I remember thinking, "God, I'm standing at the very edge of the planet's southernmost continent with nothing between me and Antarctica." When I dared to look down the face of the craggy cliff, I could see a rounded rock formation far below created by the endless waves that flowed back and forth across it for millions of years. Those softly rounded rocks were arranged in such an obvious feminine form it made me think of a fertility statue I had seen at Goddess Camp – a woman's body made up of rounded mounds (think the Paleolithic Venus figurine). And as the water kept washing back and forth over that fertility figure I remember thinking, "In Neolithic times a sight like this could instigate the genesis of religion!" If you're an Aboriginal eons ago, you'd make something of that. It just seemed to be a human thing to do. I silently thanked my sly Gray Nomad for his instructions and for wisely not telling me what to expect at the end of the path.

By the end of the day, I was at my anticipated stop at the Western Australia/South Australia border town of Eucla, where much to my amazement, I encountered a large crowd. I couldn't understand how they got there. No one had passed me on the road and yet here they were, a merry band of revelers in the middle of nowhere, all enjoying their summer holidays (Australian summer, of course, runs December through February). Due to the time change as I rode West, I arrived too early. I wasn't feeling congenial and didn't want to experience "civilization" just yet. I checked with the front desk and they gratefully refunded my money and sent me on my way, assuring me I could make the next Roadhouse before dusk. Within a few hundred yards, I found myself perched once again on a precipice not unlike the one at the Pichi Richi Pass on my second day out. Lying out in front of me was another unfathomable terrain of emptiness and to add insult to injury, dark, threatening storm clouds were going to be my afternoon companion. What had I done? Should I turn back? Never really being someone to "look back," I decided to push on and took out my fear and frustration by cursing the short craggy trees that strangely dotted only the right side of the highway.

My gamble proved correct in that not one drop of rain fell.

THAT EVENING, I ARRIVED at the Mundrabilla Roadhouse which in the local parlance was called a "hotel." In truth, it was a pub with accommodations, as were most of the local hotels. The hotel designation came about due to government regulations that would only grant liquor licenses to taverns if rooms were available. It was done in order to keep drunks from getting on the road after a heavy night of drinking.

The Mundrabilla Roadhouse had a warm and friendly atmosphere. I sat at the counter talking, ironically, with a fellow named Geoff – last name Mason – and his buddy, Spider. They were part of a permanent crew that was always on the move making road repairs. They lived in trailers and set up encampments creating makeshift towns that would pop up and disappear as they moved along the Nullarbor. As we were knocking back a few beers, the publican (barkeep) came up to me and said, "Are you Lindy?" I said, "I'm Linda." He said, "Close enough. There's a phone call for you." I knew right away it was my Geoff. The barkeep showed me to a phone in the back storeroom and I sat down on the floor behind the beer kegs and hugged the phone to my ear. The first words out of my mouth were, "How'd you find me?"

Geoff knew that frequently in his country the only telephone in Outback towns was at the hotel. He had spent the day trying to locate me in one roadhouse after another until he found me. I was so excited to tell him about what I had seen that I just began spouting off about everything. He listened to me babble on and finally said "I bet there were plenty times you thought to yourself, 'What the hell am I doing here?'." By that time, I was feeling very sure of myself and replied, "No Geoff, it was just the opposite. I thought to myself how lucky I am to be here." I may have doubted my sanity early in the trip, but now I was already more than halfway there. Turning back now was not an option.

In tracking me down, Geoff had spoken to the hotel guy in Eucla who remembered me coming through earlier in the day. Like the seasoned biker he was, Geoff asked if any other motorcyclists were camped there. The Eucla guy said, "Yeah there are two fellas on Moto Guzzis and a married couple on one BMW." Geoff's advice to me was, "Don't get ahead of yourself. Take your time and let these people catch up to you so you'll have companions to ride with." He was reading my mind. Despite my display of confidence, I still had to travel the enormous expanse across the Nullarbor Plains and I was starting to feel the enormity of the trip. I knew the remainder of the journey could be difficult if I was all on my own.

Early the next morning I said goodbye to my new friends, Geoff and Spider, and promised I would try to see them again on the way back. The motorcyclists I was waiting for hadn't yet shown up, but I wanted to be on the move and decided I could take it slow until they caught up with me. A few miles down the road I was heading for a petrol station when I spotted another Australian oddity. Standing all by itself in the middle of nowhere, was one lone tree. Nullarbor (null arbor) means no trees in Latin, so to see a tree in this barren landscape was quite astonishing. As I got closer, I could see that there were objects hanging from the tree glinting in the morning light. I had to stop the bike and get off to make sure of what I was seeing. Tied to every branch of the tree were empty Coca Cola bottles, at least a hundred of them. Pinned on the tree was a piece of paper scrawled with the words, "A bloomin' Coca Cola Bottle Tree." The iconic Aussie sense of humor was everywhere.

I was filing up at the petrol station when my expected companions arrived. As Geoff had described them John and Ian, the two Moto Guzzi motorcyclists, were on their way to try to get work at the Kalgoorlie mines in Western Australia and the other couple, Emma and Nick, on one BMW K bike, were school teachers off on their summer holiday. At first, Nick was the driver but at every other stop they switched places. So, Emma was also a biker and not just a "pillion," (what they call the person sitting behind the driver on a very uncomfortable little seat which is known as "the pillion seat").

We immediately became friends and rode tandem until we came to a crossroad town called Norseman. We weren't that far from Kalgoorlie (180km / 117 mi) and even though there was a storm coming in, everybody wanted to get to their destination. We took a vote and rather than stay in Norseman, which had a perfectly good motel, we decided to venture on. No sooner had we turned North to Kalgoorlie than we were swamped by the worst rainstorm any of us had ever encountered. At one point, we could barely see the bike in front of us. Finally, the teacher, Nick, slowed us all down and we gathered together in the pouring rain and agreed we should turn back to a milk bar in the one-horse-town of Widiemooltha, we had passed a few miles back. We made it there to discover the only shelter was the porch of a flimsy shed next to the store. We stood there shivering for almost an hour until the storm finally subsided and we took off again, soaked to the skin. It was a scary experience and I was grateful to have companions.

Australia always has some surprise in store and we were in for a big one. The storm had filled the sky with dark clouds much of the day. We hadn't seen daylight for many hours and it seemed as if night had already fallen. Then unexpectedly, on the western horizon the setting sun broke through the clouds spilling a silver light across the sky unlike anything I had ever witnessed. It was silver, pure shimmering silver.

We rode on in awe of the profound experience we had shared. In Kalgoorlie we said our goodbyes and went our separate ways. John and Ian went off to the mines, Nick and Emma headed for the nearest campsite, and I checked into the best hotel I could find. Kalgoorlie was bone dry and hadn't seen a drop of water in two years. I was still completely soaked to the skin. In fact, I squished into the hotel lobby. Nobody mentioned it, but I could see from their stares that these people hadn't seen a storm victim in a long time.

A hot shower and dinner revived me and the next morning I got my map out and confirmed that in about five hours I would be in Perth. It was January 18th; I'd been on the road five days. As I traveled those last few hundred miles, I could see civilization returning and looking very similar to other parts of Australia. When I reached the inner suburb of Shenton Park where the Rourkes lived, about twelve miles out of downtown Perth, I decided to stop at a milk bar to get some specific directions to Philomena's house on Rosalee Street. I got off the bike, looked up at the corner street sign, and there it was – Rosalee Street.

Number 18 turned out to be the first house on the left and I pulled straight into her driveway. I was covered head to toe with bugs and dirt from the trip and must have looked like an alien. I had no idea if I would even recognize Philomena. I had only met her once, and it had been six months earlier. All of a sudden, I looked to my right and there was a car coming along from the opposite direction. I was sure it was Philomena and it was clear she wanted to know what was going on in her driveway. I gave her this one-minute finger sign and took off my helmet. She rolled the window down and as I stumbled toward the car. She said, "Linda what the hell are you doing here?"

Yes, it's true. She wasn't expecting me – didn't even know I was coming. I didn't let her know in advance because even though she was the reason for my journey, she wasn't the purpose. I didn't want to call her because if she wasn't going to be there I didn't want to know. I had to have a reason to make that trip and she was it. So, after she said, "Linda what the hell are you doing here?" I burst into tears, "Philomina, I have never felt so far away in my whole life." She took a long look at me and said, "How about a beer and a spa?" That was the best offer I'd heard in five days. She showed me where the nice Jacuzzi bathtub was, handed me a beer and left me alone. I slipped into the bubbling hot water, raised my beer in a toast, and said, "Congratulations Linda, you made it!"

CHAPTER 18

Damn Willy Willy

1990-1991

The two days I spent in Perth with Philomena Rourke, her husband, Bryan, and their two children were just what I needed. Like most Australians, they were extremely hospitable and loved showing off their country. They gave me the complete Perth tour and introduced me to their circle of friends who were all impressed with my journey and made me feel quite the celebrity. As the time came for my departure, I began to have anxieties about the return trip. I couldn't help but reflect on all I had come through to get to Perth. Could I do it all over in reverse? There was another option; the bike and I could go back by train and avoid all the rigors we had previously encountered. I had to make my decision before I returned to that infamous four-way stop at Norseman, the western gateway to the Nullarbor. I decided to wait until I got to that crossroad.

After calculating the number of days it would take me to get back to Melbourne and the date when Geoff would be arriving, I decided that there was enough time to take a scenic side trip down the southern coast of Western Australia. I stopped in the beach towns of Busselton and Northcliffe to admire the great views of the ocean and to marvel at the amazing Tuart trees (Eucalyptus Gomphocephala) that looked like giant stalks of broccoli. Among numerous highlights and encounters two stood out as most memorable. First was my sighting of a kangaroo contemplating a road crossing; luckily for me it decided to make a complete

180 degree turn and headed back to the safety of the bush. Second was a quick stop on the side of the road to pull out my sunglasses as the morning cloud cover had lifted. Because it required removing my helmet, I had the unexpected experience of no sound. When I say no sound, I mean NO ambient sound! What I could hear was my own breathing and, I think, blood circulation. It was so eerie and unnerving that I decided to shuffle my feet in the dirt when lo and behold I uncovered a flattened white beer can labeled "1983 America's Cup." That yacht race had taken place in Freemantle, Western Australia and won by the *Australia II* of the Royal Perth Yacht Club. That beer can is still in my possession, proudly displayed, complete with grit, sand, and Outback soil.

After one lonely overnight in the town of Denmark, I headed for Norseman arriving in time for dinner. In the one and only restaurant, there was me and a family of four – a mother, father, and their son and daughter, both under ten. Not surprisingly the family quickly invited me to join them. Introductions made, I was then quizzed about my being in Norseman. I gave them the one-minute version probably sounding a bit down in the mouth. Their immediate reaction was one of awe and excitement. "How amazing of you!" The pep talk continued straight through the evening with a nightcap at their camp site. After saying our goodbyes when I returned to the motel, I couldn't help notice my spirits had lifted considerably. It was then that the decision to remain calm, get a good night's rest, and after breakfast and bike packing, take a bit longer at the four-way stop sign and decide between my two return options... take a left, head north to the Kalgoorlie train station... or... head straight (due east) and cross the bloody desert again. With clutch pulled in and nervous revving of the throttle, my mind went something like this: There would be a day of reckoning; telling Dennis Casey of my exploits, I would have to admit taking the train back to Melbourne. Echoing in my brain was Dennis's reaction, "What? You only rode it one way?" That was it. I took a deep breath, slowly released the clutch and twisted the throttle – one way was never an option.

Surprisingly, the return trip was much easier than I anticipated. Perhaps because I already knew the terrain or perhaps because waiting for me at the end of this journey would be the man I loved. For most of the ride back, I was on my own. The only other motorcyclists I encountered were going in the opposite direction. I did get a lot of waving and horn honking from "road trains," those giant three, sometimes four cabs long, 18-wheelers that cruise the highway day and night. Their noisy greetings always made me feel that somehow the drivers knew who I was and were expecting to see me. That notion was confirmed when I arrived in Mundrabilla and once again met up with Geoff Mason and Spider who confirmed they had sent out word on CB radio for all the "trains" to look out for me. There it was — evidence of the unseen biker watch network in action.

Once I left Mundrabilla, I did connect with a couple of other riders. The first was Taz, an Army guy on a Kawasaki. We rode along together for the next couple of days until we came to Port Augusta where he went north to Alice Springs and I continued on for a few more miles. The heat was so intense, it felt like it was frying my head off and the cylinder on the right side of the bike was cooking my foot inside my boot. It became so bad that I had to keep straightening my leg away from the bike in order to get some relief. I knew I needed some help.

A couple of days prior, a man and a young boy in a truck had stopped to talk to me at a petrol station. The man was a motorcyclist and in the best biker fashion he let me know that if I ran into any trouble I could call on him. That kind of instant camaraderie is one of the things I loved the most about biking. He handed me his business card which I tucked away thinking I would never need it. But now I did need it. I needed to get off my bike for a day or so and cool down. I was far from any major civilization, but a quick call to the number and I knew everything would be okay. The young boy answered the phone. His parents weren't home, but he gave me instructions on how to get there and told me he would call them and let them know I was coming. It was one of those little miracles of the road that I was learning to accept as the norm.

I arrived at their house where the boy's parents eagerly greeted me. As it turned out, everyone else was suffering from the heat as well. The family set me up in their guest room and suggested we all take a trip to the community pool. It sounded like heaven… and it was. Splashing in the cool water with all the other locals felt like the most natural thing to do. By the end of the day, I felt like myself again. Those people were like angels to me and gave me exactly what I needed at a crucial time. The next morning, they even made breakfast for me before sending me on my way. All I could think of as I rode off was how a random act of kindness can restore your faith in humanity.

Two hours down the highway, I picked up a travel companion, actually two companions; a couple from Ireland who were on one bike. We rode alongside each other appreciating the camaraderie for about thirty minutes until we spotted a roadside bar/hotel. With a mutual nod, we decided to grab a bite and get to know each other. Once we had stripped off our head gear, I was stunned by the couple. They were two of the most gorgeous people I have ever seen – he with dark curly hair and green eyes and she with a porcelain complexion and typical Irish auburn hair. The lilting music of their Irish accent was like a drink of cool water. What I learned was they were biking across Australia for a year and camping out everywhere. They hadn't stayed a single night in a hotel. When I thought about my often sparse accommodations that at least provided me with a bed and shower, I was humbled by their commitment. They were nearing the end of their journey and the red and brown colors of Australia had become too much for them. The one thing they hungered for was to see some Eire emerald green.

They were good riding buddies for a short while, but by the time I reached Adelaide I was all on my own again and fighting a terrible wind off the Southern Fleurieu Peninsula that twice blew me clear across the road. I had it in my mind to take a ferry to Kangaroo Island, but the windy conditions moored the ferry. I headed for a previously visited town of Hahndorf. Thankfully, that was the last of my trials. On Friday the 26th of January 1991, I checked into the Hepburn Springs Hotel, where Geoff and I had been the previous October on the Weekend Escape Tour. It never occurred to me then, that I would be back again so soon and under such unimaginable circumstances. I spent the rest of the day reading and napping in the charming corner room I had booked for our rendezvous, but my every thought was on the next day when Geoff would arrive.

Hepburn Springs was only an hour and half out of Melbourne and Geoff was scheduled to meet me there mid-day. On Saturday morning, I relaxed with a wonderful massage and at 1 p.m. Geoff arrived looking more handsome than ever. It had only been two weeks since we last saw each other, but it seemed like a lifetime. I knew the many challenges I had gone through and was certain that Geoff had faced his own trials with his wife, Maxine. His smiling face confirmed that a great weight had been lifted off his shoulders. He now wore his wedding ring on his right hand. It was a small gesture that signaled a big change. He wrapped his arms around me and we held tight to each other. That comforting embrace reassured me that we were ready to move ahead with our lives.

The following day Geoff went to the airport in Melbourne to pick up the clients for the next Mulga Tour. I would join them at lunchtime in Sovereign Hill and I took the afternoon off to write my daughter Maida a long letter. I had a lot of explaining to do.

MAIDA HAD EVERY RIGHT to know how serious my relationship was with Geoff. She was a loving daughter who had real concerns about my happiness. She knew I was still emotionally connected to Larry and how deeply it affected me when I learned that Larry was seriously involved with a woman named Joyce. I was well aware of who Joyce was. She owned a business that organized big meetings for companies like Schwab. She wore lots of pancake makeup, tons of gold jewelry, and a stiff, severe hairdo. She was a woman who was nothing like me.

During those endless days on the road, I'd had time to think long and hard about Larry and his behavior for the past couple of years. On a phone call to Maida, I finally got up the nerve to say, "I wonder if in fact, Joyce was there all along and I just didn't know it." Her answer was, "Duh?" As it turned out, Maida had already confronted Larry asking, "Was Joyce around before you and Mom split up?" He, of course, denied it but Maida said,

"Mom, he's lying." I knew she was right. Joyce had been in the picture for some time.

"Do you think it's going to last?" I asked Maida. She laughed and said, "He'll never admit he made a mistake a second time. And he definitely won't want to split everything down the middle again."

It was a conversation that made me re-examine my thinking and realize that Larry had hung in there those last few years not because he was trying to salvage our marriage, but because he was trying to figure out how to not give me half of everything we owned. For my part, I was so steeped in my own personal struggle I didn't really give much thought to our financial situation. I knew we were well off and could afford to live a comfortable life, but our actual monetary worth was never disclosed to me.

When it came time for the divorce, we were both so ready to be done with it we had one lawyer represent both of us and the only skirmish we had was over one lamp and one chair. I took the lamp; he took the chair. Why drag things out? I had this Australian guy I was crazy about halfway 'round the world and I was happy to get the divorce over and done. All I wanted was enough of a financial cushion to keep living a fairly comfortable life. I had no idea what we were worth. I never knew what Larry's salary was and I certainly didn't know what our stock portfolio looked like. At one point in our marriage, Larry and I had gone to a financial manager, Christopher Croft, who was supposed to help us diversify our assets, but Larry never followed the plan. Larry's idea was, "I'll just keep Schwab going and we'll keep everything in one pot." When the crash happened in '87 I thought to myself, "That's not such a good idea. We need to spread our money around." At the time, I didn't have any financial acumen, so I put the idea on a back burner.

After the divorce Larry said to me, "You're going to need a financial planner; you should hire Christopher Croft." Despite our divorce, I still trusted Larry. I called Chris Croft and said, "Larry and I are done. Whatever I'm left with I want to make sure we spread it around so I'm not just relying on Schwab to keep the bankroll going." Chris agreed and we scheduled a meeting.

I dressed in my most business-like pantsuit and entered Chris's office feeling very grown up. I was a woman in her forties who was about to take financial control of her life. I had no idea what Chris had in store for me. For the first time, I learned how much money Larry and I had amassed in our twenty-three years of marriage – you could have knocked me over with a feather – the sum was substantial. Chris went over the details of how he would invest the funds in different stocks and bonds to ensure that I would be well taken care of for the rest of my life. Two thoughts crossed my mind: one, a resentment that Larry had made me put my hand out every two weeks for a household allowance when all this money was just sitting there; and two, the realization that I would never need to fly coach again.

FOR THE NEXT EIGHTEEN MONTHS, I traveled back and forth from Australia to the U.S. establishing a bi-hemispheric life that I would lead for at least the next two decades. I had close ties to my friends in San Francisco and Maida was continuing her college education in Southern California, so it seemed logical to maintain a residence in the Bay Area. I purchased a small Marina-style house on Culebra Terrace and started in on the renovations which had to be carried on by FAX when I was in Australia.

Geoff and I were now fully committed to each other, but neither of us was ready to talk about marriage, so we decided to get a place together in Australia. He promised to look around for something while I was off on a short trip to America. On my return, I discovered he had made absolutely no progress on the housing front. For all his amazing skills, finding a place for us to live was beyond him. All his life, Geoff had depended on women to take care of domestic matters. He didn't know where to begin with something that wasn't pertinent to Mercedes or motorcycles. I took note of that, but it didn't faze me. I simply started looking for something suitable and quickly found a small two-bedroom one-story cinderblock unit, not far from the BMW dealership. The size was adequate and the price was right so I signed the lease and started fixing it up.

Geoff was supportive of whatever I wanted to do. I soon found myself dividing my time between decorating the modest, postage-stamp sized rental, renovating the San Francisco property and helping Geoff in the office – booking tours and promoting the company. It was a wonderfully happy time. Not only was I involved in my own creative projects, I was enjoying a partnership with a man I was in love with.

Geoff's ambition was to take his company to prominence in the motorcycle world. I encouraged him to expand his small fleet of bikes, to reach out to foreign clients, and increase his advertising budget. These all came with a hefty cost. It was well worth the happy life we were leading.

When you're in love – or in lust – you overlook a lot of things that in hindsight you should have paid more attention to. Early on, I could see that Geoff's motorcycle business didn't have much chance of success. The main problem was that Americans, who were the prime audience for this kind of tour, generally didn't have enough vacation time to come to Australia for the number of days a decent tour would take. The Australians only did the short weekend trips because either they couldn't afford to do a longer trip or if they had their own bikes, they believed they could do an extended trip on their own – they didn't need an Australian guiding them. I didn't see any clear way around this problem and neither did Geoff. But that didn't stop us from trying.

I must admit, I actually liked the Weekend Escape tours. Often it would be wives who had seen the advertisement in a local motorcycle magazine and would book the trip saying, "I want to get us a three-day trip because he gave up his motorcycle when we got married and I had the baby." It was a way of showing their husbands some love and I was all for that. I met a lot of great Australians that way and even if those short trips weren't financially successful, they were fun for me. I know they were fun for Geoff, too.

What I began to see was that part of Geoff's way of moving through life was to be a Pollyanna. One of his favorite expressions was, "Well, let's just let AMT pay for it." I was perturbed by that attitude because I knew the company had no money and basically it was me paying for everything, but the benefits I was deriving overruled practicality. Admittedly, there were some moments that made us believe that Geoff's dream was viable, for example, when a motorcycle entrepreneur from Austria named Werner Wachter entered our lives.

Werner was a charming and interesting fellow who ran his own motorcycle travel company, Edelweiss Bike Tours. He, along with a group of German motorcyclists, had done a long trip with us and he was so impressed by Geoff that he invited him to become part of his worldwide roster of bike tour guides. We went into business with Werner and developed a very amicable relationship with him and his British wife, Carol. Our first tour with them took us out of Australia to the Swiss Alps. It was a big success and both Geoff and I were excited to be exploring new territory. As a result of our affiliation with Edelweiss, we did get more customers for our Oz tours, mostly English, German, Austrian, and Dutch, but still very few Americans. We were barely able to cover our expenses, but it kept us in business and Werner was always enthusiastic and upbeat about the future.

By the time a year passed, I had become an integral part of Geoff's company. I would greet new clients and take them on a short introductory bike run around Melbourne so I could get a bead on who were the better riders and who was going to need some watching over. I would come back and report to Geoff about who I thought should go where in our formation. Geoff was always in front in the lead position and we'd put the weakest people behind him. I would be the last person, bringing up the rear and keeping an eye on the whole group. We were working together as a team and had all our logistics well planned in order to make the experience as smooth and memorable as possible.

Getting any new group out of the city was a challenge because to them it seemed that everybody was riding on the wrong side of the road (unless they were from England or Japan). Once we made it out of town, we would stop for a coffee break and everyone would start to relax. Things got a lot easier once we were in the Bush and headed off on our established route. Our first stop was the Gold Country where we would spend the night. Because we were repeat customers, we were always given a big welcome wherever we stopped and our group was given the royal treatment. It was that kind of personal touch that made our trips so special. The next morning it would be breakfast and "clutches out" at 9 a.m. – meaning you had to be at your bike and ready to go on the dot. Geoff and I had worked everything out so seamlessly that it all became fairly routine. There was very little that was new or unexpected – until one morning in March of 1991, almost eighteen months after I first set foot in Australia.

This particular tour had been booked in conjunction with Edelweiss and we had one of our bigger crowds including a Canadian, a couple of Americans, and a group of Germans. The trip began routinely. On our second day out, we were heading toward the Pichi Richi Pass – that great "beauty spot" where I had first seen the vastness of Australia. The Canadian, who was quite a photographer, saw that we were coming into some spectacular scenery. He wanted to stop for some photos. Geoff said, "I'll hang back with him and let him take some pictures. Why don't you and the rest of the folks go on up to the Pichi Richi café and we'll meet you there?" I was happy to keep moving and headed off with the rest of the group.

We were all enjoying a hot cup of coffee at the café when a truck driver came up to our table and said, "Which one of you is Linda?" I said, "That's me, I'm Linda." "Well one of your blokes had an accident about ten or fifteen miles up the road and you need to go back." My initial reaction was that it couldn't possibly be Geoff, but I quickly asked, "Was it the Canadian or the Australian?" "Yeah," he answered, "It was the Australian."

Without even zipping up my jacket I got on my bike and told the others to stay put. I barreled down the road, my mind racing with fear, praying that the truck driver had been wrong, that it wasn't Geoff. But when I pulled up to where a knot of people were gathered at the side of the road and jumped off my bike, there he was lying prone at the bottom of a gully. What remained of his bike lay yards away in a culvert, unrecognizable; twisted, the handlebars caved in. It didn't look anything like a motorcycle. I remember someone saying an ambulance was on the way and I scrambled down the gully to help them get his helmet off without damaging his spine. Geoff had obviously been thrown off his bike, but thank God, he was still alive. By the time I reached him he was gasping for air and his eyes were darting all over the place. When he heard my voice, he tried to speak, but it all came out in gibberish. I tried to get him into consciousness, but couldn't. Worst of all, no one knew what had happened. No one had witnessed anything. The last thing the Canadian recalled was Geoff saying, "You look like you'll be okay on your own, I'm just gonna' tootle on up to the Pichi Richi and hang out with Linda and the rest of them. Take your time taking pictures." The next thing he saw was Geoff's smashed bike lying on the roadside and Geoff in a gully by the side of the road.

There was no evidence the bike had been hit by another vehicle and the only reasonable answer anyone could think of was that he had been taken down by what we call Willy Willy's – dust devils – mini tornados that come up after two or three o'clock in the afternoon – they do their thing, blinding a biker and then disappear. In Australia, they are known to have overturned eighteen wheelers, so it's not unheard of that something like that could have happened. It was the only logical conclusion anyone could come to. Geoff had no memory of what happened.

GRATEFULLY, AN AMBULANCE ARRIVED. With me following on my motorcycle we ended up in a rural hospital in Whyalla – a distance of 88.55 km (55.02 mi.) Whylla was the windy town I had avoided on my way to Perth. Geoff was immediately taken to intensive care while I sat in the hospital lobby with no information for what seemed like forever. I was in a state of shock and I don't know how I did it, but somehow, I got the Canadian fellow on the phone and managed to juggle the rest of the tour from the hospital.

Maida was expecting my return to San Francisco the following week and I called to let her know about the accident. Her supportive response was, "Mom, he needs you more than I do at this point." She was right. Geoff was in intensive care for at least two weeks before he was deemed in stable condition. Physically, he was in great pain from emergency surgery that had been performed on his leg and mentally he was still in a fog. He recognized me, but continued to babble incoherently and had no awareness of anything going on around him. I knew from my nursing experience he was in for a long, painful rehab and the prognosis for returning to his former self was not good.

My knight in shining armor, my hero, the man I had planned a wonderful new life with was now lying before me bandaged and broken, hooked to machines, his mind adrift. I searched for some familiar sign: a twinkle in his eyes, a devilish smile, or any trace of the cheerful personality that had won my heart. They were all gone. I looked at the damaged shell of what was once my beloved Geoff Coat and the only thing I could think was how my entire world had come crashing down.

CHAPTER 19

Reality in Russia

1991-1993

Some people say that L. Frank Baum wrote *The Wizard of Oz* after glimpsing from afar, the Emerald City of Perth. I had a similar reaction the first time I witnessed that sparkling city on my solo adventure. I remember thinking how magical it appeared shimmering in the distance and how fitting it was that all of Australia had become known as Oz. Now, more than ever, it seemed appropriate for my circumstances. I was definitely far from home in a land called Oz and, like Dorothy, all I could think of was how to get back to the world I once knew.

Geoff had been in such good physical shape before the accident that his body healed relatively quickly. His mind? That was another story. The hospital in Whyalla couldn't give him the kind of care I thought he should have. He was in ICU for two weeks and the minute he was out, I managed with great difficulty, to fly him home. Once we were back in our Melbourne apartment, it was like living in a psycho ward. Geoff was spouting gibberish and making bizarre pronouncements: "I want to cure all the hunger in the world;" "I want to watch every sunset that ever happens." He needed constant attention and his medications required continual monitoring and adjusting. I knew his unsettling behavior was due to the head trauma he had suffered and it would take time for him to start thinking logically. As if playing nursemaid wasn't hard enough, I also had to take care of the next Mulga Tour which was going out in less than a month.

Maybe I was taking on more than I could handle, but it was such a day-to-day process I didn't have time to think it through. I just got to work and got on with it the best could. I had been a nurse, I was familiar with patient care, so at least I knew where to look for help. Nearby, I found a nursing facility where Geoff would get twenty-four-hour-a-day care and I could maintain phone contact with him while I fulfilled the tour company obligation. To help with the tour, I called on Geoff's nineteen-year-old son, John, a seasoned motorcyclist. He would help with driving a support vehicle towing his dirt bike and offer a true Aussie presence for authenticity.

Among the many skills Geoff had lost in the accident was his ability to tell time. Ironically, he was an expert watchmaker who had taught himself how to fix watches while he was in Vietnam and had taken a master course in watchmaking upon his return home. After the accident, he could still look at a watch and tell you what was wrong with it, but he couldn't read the time. It was one of the inexplicable side effects of his brain injury. While I was out on the Mulga Tour, I made a habit of calling Geoff every morning and every afternoon. Somehow that helped him get back in touch with the concept of time. At some point, he started gushing to the nurses that he was excited because Linda would be calling soon. Little by little, he began to get back some of the abilities he had lost. He was making good progress at the nursing facility and they agreed he could be released when I returned from the tour.

THE TOUR WENT EXCEEDINGLY well. It was a particularly compatible group which included a few Americans, one of them was a sweet Jewish guy from Chicago named Burt Richmond. I'd grown up with a lot of kind, Jewish men in the New York/New Jersey area and I had an affinity for them. Burt was cute and charming with a devilish twinkle in his eye. He was an architect and a designer so right away we had a lot in common. His wife was with him on the trip, so there was no romantic involvement, but we really hit it off as friends. At some point on that trip Burt confessed that he was actually there to spy on our operation because he was running Lotus

Tours, a similar motorcycle touring company out of Chicago. I was more than happy to share information with him and that became the beginning of a friendship that would eventually have a great impact on my life.

At the end of every tour, the clients were required to bring their motorcycles back to the storage space we called our "corporate headquarters" in Collingwood. Inevitably clients, especially on the longer trips, would become closely bonded and this group was no different. As they surrendered their bikes back to Australian Motorcycle Touring (AMT), they chattered away with the kind of euphoria that comes as a result of having mutually experienced an exciting adventure. I always enjoyed sharing that final day with the clients and watching them leave energized and satisfied with the tour. I was in the midst of the last-minute details, making sure that all the equipment had been returned in good condition, when there was a sudden change in the atmosphere. I turned to see a figure standing in the doorway. It was Geoff, probably fifteen pounds lighter and a mere shadow of himself. At the sight of him my heart leapt with joy and I realized how much I had been missing him. I wanted to rush to him and jump into his arms. I wanted him to whisper in my ear how proud he was that I had pulled off a great tour without the clients ever knowing about his accident or how much emotional pain I was in. But at the same time, I didn't want to blow my cool in front of the clients, so I just stood there grinning like a foolish child desperately in need of a pat on the head. Imagine my despair when Geoff walked right past me with no sign of recognition. I watched him greet the clients as if I didn't exist. All he could focus on was playing his role as the CEO of the Australian Motorcycle Touring Company. He had no clue who these people were, but it was important to him to shake their hands and say, "Sorry I couldn't make it. Thank you very much for being a client. Is there anything else we can do for you?" Then I recalled seeing my sister go through the same kind of forced behavior after her accident — pretending to be normal when it was obvious something inside her head was very wrong. I knew then that even though Geoff was trying hard to act like his old self, he was far from it.

The next few months were sheer chaos as I worried over Geoff's condition and struggled to keep AMT alive. We had trips scheduled to go out every three weeks and in between I was doing my best to deal with Geoff's recovery. We tried counseling with a young woman therapist. Geoff had no respect for her and was uncooperative. She in turn threatened to take away the multi-vehicle driver's licenses he kept from his military days – probably the last thing she should have done. It was a disaster. That was the end of the therapist. Sticking to a pre-accident plan, I decided what we needed was a new place to live. Maybe it was because in our little apartment I felt that Geoff was on top of me, following me around like a needy puppy. Or maybe I was heeding some ancient nesting call, "Change your place, change your life."

I found a bigger place on Canning Street, North Carlton, which turned out to be ideal. We had enough furniture from the old place to make it comfortable and once I got Geoff settled and was confident he could take care of himself, I decided what I needed was a trip to America. I knew I wanted to see Maida and I needed some space where I could feel like myself again.

IN SAN FRANCISCO, surrounded by people I loved, I realized my devotion to Geoff and my determination to see him through his recovery were taking a serious toll on me. Part of me still held on to the belief that one day the man I so madly loved would magically return to his old self and we would pick up where we had left off. But another more realistic part of me recognized that even if his body and mind healed completely, the light-hearted, confident Geoff I had fallen in love with, had been permanently changed. I wasn't sure what kind of man he was becoming or what that would mean to our relationship.

I returned to Melbourne in time for the next scheduled tour. Geoff seemed to have handled my being away in San Francisco well enough. In fact, he was planning to take part in the next tour which I encouraged him to do. I didn't know whether I was pushing Geoff too hard or that

I believed work was great therapy. The truth was, neither of us knew exactly what we were doing. We were both marching along the best we could. But now I could see that Geoff too wanted desperately to get back to what we once had.

We were now full partners with Edelweiss. They had taken over most of the tour organizing while Geoff and I took care of the actual running of the tours. There was no question that Geoff was physically up to the task, but cracks in his personality had begun to appear and his once remarkably even temper had grown short. One of the things I most admired about Geoff was his uncanny ability to always know where he was geographically. He operated by sheer instinct and never needed a map. One of the significant changes I saw in him after the accident was a diminished sense of direction and a kind of confusion about where he was. I knew that had to be a major blow to Geoff's ego. It's hard for any man who's been at the top of his game to accept the lessening of his abilities. The fact that it happened prematurely as the result of an accident made it even harder. Especially for someone running a tour company!

Things began to unravel noticeably on an Edelweiss tour with a group from Japan. I was only going to be able to take part in the first day of the trip because I had arranged an automobile trip around Australia for my financial advisor, Christopher Croft, and his daughter. I told Geoff I was going to leave after the first day of the Edelweiss tour to get Chris and his daughter settled and I would rejoin him after a few days. Geoff was feeling well enough to handle things on his own – or so he said. I should have known better. I was aware that Geoff harbored ill feelings toward the Japanese related to what happened during the Second World War. The Japanese had forced war prisoners, among them many Australians, to participate in brutal "death marches." One of those captives was Geoff's stepfather who suffered from what we now call PTSD. He vented his pent-up fury in physical attacks on both Geoff and his mother. This trauma affected Geoff's view of our Japanese tourists who were just out for a good time.

Even on his best day, an eleven-day trip with Japanese tourists was probably not something Geoff was eager to do, but he made no mention of it. I did as I promised; I got Christopher and his daughter launched on their road trip and went back to meet up with Geoff and his tour group. By the time I returned, Geoff had had it with the Japanese and was barely holding on. It wasn't that he couldn't do the job. He could get them to the various lunch and dinner spots and get them to their motels, but his attitude toward the clients was brusque and unfriendly. I don't know what they thought was happening. Being Japanese, they were very polite about everything. But I must say they were glad to see me return.

That night after dinner I sat Geoff down for a serious talk about our future. When I asked him, "Do you want to ever do this again?" Without hesitation, he said. "No." I knew that was the beginning of the end of Austrailian Motorcycle Touring.

～

THE HARDEST PART WAS telling Werner. Our partnership had worked out well for him. He had made a deal with Geoff to get his cut off the top. Even I, who didn't know all that much about business, tried to steer Geoff away from that arrangement. I wanted them to split the difference. Geoff, like many Australians, was very nice and not as cutthroat as he should have been in negotiating contracts. Werner had prevailed and the deal had worked to his advantage, not ours.

The next day I sent a fax to Werner in Austria to say, "It's over." He called right away wanting to know "What? Why?" I said, "It's done Werner; there's no way Geoff wants or has the ability to do this ever again." Werner and I were good friends and he begged me to keep the tours going, but in my heart, I knew it was over. It didn't mean that Geoff and I wouldn't continue participating in motorcycle tours; it just meant that AMT wouldn't be organizing them or leading them. Once Werner accepted our decision, I started the grim work of dismantling the company.

The first thing I had to do was acknowledge that I knew nothing about numbers; basically, I was afraid of them. I'd always found comfort in learning new things, but my basic nature was geared towards flexibility and freedom — the antithesis of numbers. Numbers were too rigid, too precise. I had seen how numbers had shut Larry down and taken all the *joie de vivre* out of him. Now I was faced with a challenge unlike any I had ever taken on – one that would force me to step outside my comfort zone and learn something difficult that I had no real desire to learn. I started by sitting down with our accountant and saying, "I want to see everything on paper. I want to know exactly what's coming in and what's going out." My greatest fear was that one day Geoff would wake up and say, "What happened to my company?" I wanted documentation to justify everything I was doing, including why we were separating from Edelweiss.

As soon as I received the report from our accountant it became obvious – between the upkeep of the bikes, the insurance and the marketing and promotion – there was no way this company was ever going to make any money. Once Werner received his cut off the top there was not much left to cover our costs. Both Geoff and I knew my money had been keeping the company afloat. I was fine with that because I loved him and I loved the potential of the company. Having never run a business before I paid little attention to the bottom line and held fast to the dream that one day AMT would be financially independent. I ignored what I should have paid careful attention to since I was the company's major investor. I really had no excuse. What would the women at Goddess Camp have said? *Caveat emptor.*

I KNEW THAT CLOSING AMT would be difficult for Geoff. In his heart, he was still a biker who loved touring, so I proposed a plan. During the Australian winter, we could live in America and explore my country. We had biker friends all over the East Coast, Mississippi, the Northwest. It would be a great chance to meet up with them again and discover places neither of us had ever been. Geoff liked the idea, and I was happy to see him enthusiastic about something. I was excited by the prospect of starting a new and promising phase of our lives.

Despite our business break up, our friendship with Werner continued. Geoff and I were part of his inner circle of professional motorcyclists and in 1992 after the collapse of the Soviet Union, Edelweiss Tours became the first Western motorcycle company allowed into Russia. Geoff and I were invited to participate in that ground-breaking tour. Our group consisted of me (the only female), Geoff, five Americans, and one German. None of us had ever traversed this foreign terrain which was fraught with potentially hazardous conditions. I knew this would be a true test of Geoff's skill level. Would he be able to step up in the ways he once did? Would his unerring instincts kick in to guide us in this new and unknown territory? These were some of the questions that I hoped would be answered over the next two weeks.

We entered Russia via Hungary into Ukraine. Our itinerary would take us north through the Russian countryside to Moscow and west to St. Petersburg where we would make our exit into Finland. Along the way we would travel through small towns and villages or stop for a night's stay in local accommodations. It promised to be quaint and charming, but we were all prepared to encounter great disparity between our Western lifestyle and what we saw in Russia. That truth was confirmed by our first night's stay in the Ukrainian town of Ternopil. We were booked into what had been described as "a relatively new Russian hotel." The elevator was only big enough for two people and a small amount of luggage. When the doors opened onto our floor we found ourselves in complete darkness. Despite the fact that Ternopil was known for manufacturing industrial light bulbs, there was no lighting in the hallways, and we had to feel our way along the walls to find our rooms. Once Geoff and I were inside our bare-bones room, we discovered that the bathroom sink was missing a section of pipe. When you washed your hands or brushed your teeth the water ran out the drain directly onto your feet. So much for the "relatively new hotel."

The town itself did have a quaint charm with a typical square where one of the highlights was having crowds follow us around in awe. It was the first time they had ever seen Americans up close and they were as curious about us as we were about them. The food situation was another challenge, especially at lunch time, where during the entire trip we only encountered one restaurant that served lunch. Fortunately, the meals at the hotels were delicious and plentiful. We quickly learned to stuff our pockets with breakfast food in order to sustain us during the day. It was the only trip I ever lost weight on.

I constantly had my antenna up about how Geoff was doing and as far as I could see, he seemed to be handling everything well. Maybe it was because we were all in a state of semi-confusion and he didn't appear to be any different from the rest of us. The roads were terrible, often unpaved and rutted and there were no good maps for our route. Russia was in complete turmoil. Many individual towns had chosen to go back to their old names and street signs were changing so fast no maps could keep up. Instead, we had been handed stacks of Xeroxed instructions on the kind of paper that if it got heated up the whole page turned black. These hastily assembled instructions were stored in the panniers on the sides of our bikes. Often, because of the heat from the motor, they would be completely blacked out and we'd be left to figure things out for ourselves. That's when I began to notice how Geoff was backing off from his usual leadership role and was deferring to the German fellow who seemed to have a pretty good handle on how to get us where we wanted to go.

The tour was far more complicated than any we had arranged for our clients in Australia, but it was part and parcel of being the first to enter a country that had been isolated for so many years. The best part of the journey was visiting the medieval villages along the way, including one that boasted a church on every square block, all of which had been boarded up during the "cultural revolution," and were now being re-opened to enthusiastic worshippers.

Our unusual presence always brought out curious people, some of whom were eager to make contact with Westerners. In one town, we met a young boy of fifteen who was desperately holding on to the last remnants of a Soviet motorcycle culture by proudly showing us his 250cc motorbike which he had painted to simulate a race bike, complete with flames emblazoned on the sides. Then there was the twenty-something Ukrainian girl, a fashion devotee, who begged me in broken English to send her the latest issues of Australian fashion magazines. In the same crowd, we encountered an elderly German man who had lived in Russia most of his life. In his eagerness to claim himself as part of the West, he insisted on showing us photos of his children and grandchildren who lived in California.

The hardest thing to wrap our heads around was the incredible shortage of goods. One afternoon we pulled into a town square. We parked our bikes and began receiving the kind of inquisitive looks we had all become used to, when we noticed a sudden rush of activity all around us. At first, we thought it had something to do with our presence but we soon realized that all the people in the square had scurried to form a long line outside a shop. Rumor had spread that for the first time in days, the shop was about to open. There was no indication of what time or when, but obviously the townspeople thought nothing of standing in line for hours for a few eggs or a loaf of bread. One store we entered had only two items on the shelves, a container of dish detergent and empty hangers on a rack.

It was a completely different experience in Moscow which is based on medieval city constructs with the iconic bulbed turrets of the Kremlin in the center and all the streets, avenues and boulevards radiating out. Traffic lights were sparse and just suggestions, resulting in traffic jams that all great cities are plagued with. Add to the fact that with the recent collapse of the Soviet Union, Russians were newly permitted to own automobiles. Hazards were numerous — missing manhole covers, ancient slippery trolley tracks and the ever-present astonished Muscovites surrounding us wondering, "Who are these people on these amazing motorcycles?"

Everything was overblown, including our hotel, The Cosmos, which was perhaps the largest hotel I have ever been in. It was meant to be luxurious but after getting stuck in an elevator and having fellow motorcyclists' luggage stolen from the parking lot, I was looking forward to getting back to the countryside. As luck would have it, I managed to come down with a head cold and was desperate for sinus and respiratory relief before putting my helmet back on. The hotel was able to provide us with a name and address of an American clinic not too far from the hotel. Using a hotel taxi getting there was uneventful. Our instruction for returning was to just stand on a corner waving and someone, anyone would pick you up. They would take German marks or U.S. dollars and you were on your own when negotiating. Sure enough, a middle-aged man stopped almost immediately and off we went. The ride back was on a busy multi-laned two-way boulevard. At the intersection, we experienced Russian traffic rules. The normally empty lanes to the left of us started to slowly fill up directly across from the oncoming traffic line up. I remember Geoff and I glancing at each other silently wondering, "What the hell?" The minute the light changed there was this furious entanglement with cars coming directly at each other. We also got to witness first-hand how the traffic police handled motorway infractions. Standing in and amongst the sea of vehicles of all shapes and drapes, they would whip a white handkerchief out of their pocket and wave it about while pointing to the infractor. The minute eye contact was made the violator would pull beside the officer and give himself up!

The one indelible memory of St. Petersburg was of a dancing bear in a park. He wore a small red vest and hat and was an obvious tourist attraction performing his tired tricks at the urging of a small whip. It was a cheap and shabby show and a pathetic metaphor for what the "great bear" of Russia had become.

Far more entertaining was a small-town circus we encountered outside St. Petersburg where, besides the usual trapeze artists and bareback riders, I witnessed the most unique act I have ever seen. A woman entered the ring with a bevy of house cats she had trained to perform the most intricate feline gymnastics imaginable. It was so incredibly entertaining that I found myself rising to my feet to applaud her. No tigers, no lions, just housecats! To this day I marvel at that performance.

Two and a half weeks after our arrival into the former, mighty Soviet Union where we had encountered villages with no running water, horse and buggies with harnesses made from tree branches and rope, we rode north out of St. Petersburg into Finland. Instantly, we were plunked down into Western civilization with proper bike paths, convenience stores, and families out enjoying themselves. The following day, we and our bikes boarded a ship for Germany. The overnight trip had Geoff all in a tither. He couldn't find his way around so he refused to come out of our cabin until we docked in Germany. We were relieved to be back in a country where the highways were smoothly-paved and the road signs made sense. Geoff had performed well enough during the trip but relinquishing his role as leader-of-the-pack to the German was having an impact on him. I could see a troubling change come over him.

CHAPTER 20

Passive Aggression

1993-1996

If you read enough books about relationships and how they progress, you'll learn that when you're in the throes of the ooey-gooey romantic part you think it will never end. It's around eighteen to twenty months when things can start to get wobbly. It's the way humans are built – optimism, or maybe denial, is part of our survival mechanism. The only other meaningful relationship I'd ever been in was with my husband Larry so I wasn't very sophisticated about what to expect. Even before Geoff's accident, there were aspects of his personality that I was ignoring. I saw what I wanted to see, and I let other things slide.

There was one particular incident I should have recognized as a warning sign but didn't. Geoff and I were in San Francisco doing our back-and-forth hemispheric thing and were spending the summer in my marina-style house. Maida had graduated from Occidental College, and I invited her to live with us for the three months we planned to be there. Geoff was frankly annoyed by that. He never said anything specifically, but it would show up in subtle ways. I had lived with Maida long enough to know she's not a morning person but give her a cup of coffee and a bite to eat and in no time, she'd be herself again. For some reason, Geoff took great offense to this. He came at me with remarks like, "She didn't even say good morning." It was in a tone that I'd never heard him use before. I said, "Give her an hour or two and she'll be fine. Just don't take it personally." So, there I was, once again, juggling personalities in the same way I'd juggled between Larry and Maida, trying to soothe any rift that could possibly develop between them. The same way I tried to run interference between my mother and father when I was a little girl. I didn't spend a lot of time analyzing his remark because I figured it wasn't uncommon behavior when you've got children and you're trying to establish a relationship with a new man. Then I recalled that earlier that year Maida had come to visit us in Australia and stayed at a hotel near our apartment. I wanted to spend as much time with her as possible, but Geoff made comments like, "Really, she's going to come to dinner too?" It was almost like sibling rivalry and should have given me some clue to his deeper feelings. It certainly meant that Maida's visits were rather short lived. If I had been smart, I might have ended it right there because it hinted at a kind of possessiveness that I didn't want in my life.

After Geoff's accident, I found myself re-thinking everything that had gone on between us. "Is this the guy who would have appeared anyway after eighteen months, or is this a guy who's actually damaged and might get better and return to his old self?" I couldn't help but wonder what would have happened if there had been no motorcycle accident. Would our relationship have changed anyway? The questions plagued me, but I couldn't answer them. Instead, I kept thinking if we just got back to doing what we were doing it will all just sort itself out. It was a delaying tactic which allowed me to keep from making any decisions about our future. Geoff, being a sweet, pleaser-type guy did his best to play along with me, but over the next year it became harder and harder for him to fake it. The reality of what had happened to Geoff began to sink in and he started going into these depressive funks that were taking a heavy toll on him and on me.

In 1993, Werner Wachter invited us to go on a scouting tour in South Africa with the Edelweiss crew. Like the Russia trip, it was the kind of tour where you're sort of a guinea pig to try out a new territory. Werner would handpick people he felt had the time, the motorcycle skills, and the funds to participate in these exotic adventures. It was sort of an insiders' club of motorcycle enthusiasts which included my friend Burt Richmond from Chicago's Lotus Tours.

The South Africa trip was truly special, with landscapes similar to Australia and California, but rich with unique South African features like fabulous Dutch architecture, elaborate "glamping" tents in the Kalahari Desert, tours of African animal reserves, and monkeys galore that would constantly steal stuff from our tank bags.

The most memorable experience of South Africa took place in a modest hotel in the middle of nowhere where the gents had to wear jackets to dinner and the employees wore colonial garb. It was a lame attempt to give tourists a sense of the "good old days," when Dutch colonists ruled South Africa and everyone dressed for dinner. Our group with their motorcycles and biker gear were obviously a big departure from the usual guests at this remote outpost. The morning after we arrived, we were milling around the front of the hotel where a cluster of young girls – maids and kitchen workers – had gathered to take a better look at us. They kept pointing and giggling, egging each other on to some kind of mischief, until one teenage girl boldly went up to one of the men on our tour and asked if he would take her for a ride on his bike. She didn't speak any English so it was all done in mime with her pointing to the bike and then to herself and nodding eagerly. He brusquely shook his head, rejecting her request. I observed in amusement as she tried to entice one guy after another to give her a ride. One by one they either ignored her or said "No." I watched as her enthusiasm waned and a discouraged look came over her face. I felt an unexpected wave of compassion for her. Without giving it much thought, I got on my bike and said, "C'mon I'll give you a ride."

Because I was short, when I was seated on the bike my feet barely touched the ground. My tippy toes were all that kept me balanced. Before I knew what happened that young girl ran straight to me and leaped on the back of my bike before I had readied myself for the weight shift. It was only luck and all my strength that kept us from ending up in a heap on the ground. The last thing I wanted was a giddy, wiggly unpredictable teenager as a passenger, but I understood this might be a once in a lifetime experience for her. Due to the language barrier, I was unable to give her instructions on the correct way to be a "pillion;" "Wait until I tell you to climb on, hold on to my waist at all times, do not shift your weight by looking backwards or pointing." She wouldn't have understood a word anyway, so all I could do was pray that she would have the good sense to hold on tight and not do anything dumb. I took her on a few laps around the parking lot and when it seemed she'd got the hang of it I headed out onto the main road and revved up the bike for a kilometer or so to give her more of a thrill. Seated behind me and holding on tight, I could feel her heart pumping and knew her adrenaline was flowing. It occurred to me that once the ride was over I was going to need a plan on how to get her safely off the bike. When the passenger doesn't know how to shift their weight properly for the dismount, there's a great danger of tipping over. I was sure we were going to have a problem. When I got back to the parking lot I rode around in circles until I got the attention of a few of the guys and let them know they needed to be waiting when I came to a stop to catch us before she 'gazelled' off. Thankfully, about four guys understood my request and formed a two-person catching committee. It worked like a charm. She flew off the bike and into their arms and couldn't wait to run to her friends to tell them all about her thrilling experience. I got some kudos from the catchers, which was nice, but it took all my self-control not to chastise all of them for having turned her down. The ride would have been much easier for any of them. With their upper body strength and their longer legs, controlling the balance of their bikes was much simpler. But like they say about Fred Astaire and Ginger Rogers, "She did everything he did, only backwards and in high heels."

That night as I lay in bed, I reflected on what that experience might have meant to that young girl. As the only woman in the group, I felt it was my duty to set an example for younger women, to show them that females might make a difference in their lives. In the case of this black girl, living in the land of apartheid, being made to wear a ridiculous colonial costume while cleaning hotel rooms of white folks, well maybe, just maybe, that experience would empower her and give her a shred of hope for her future. Most likely, the odds were against her. All I knew for sure is that I would have never forgiven myself if we all just rode off leaving an extremely disappointed young girl ignored and dismissed. Instead, she would have a lasting remembrance of the time a foreign lady gave her a fantastic ride on a motorcycle.

FROM THE VERY BEGINNING of the South Africa trip, it had been clear that Geoff was no longer going to be the lead guy. More and more he would end up at the rear of the pack and I would find myself looking back in my rear-view mirror to keep an eye on him. One afternoon on one of those long desert stretches that often become tedious, I looked back to see Geoff weaving his bike – back and forth, back and forth, back and forth. At first, I thought he was just playing around; then I recognized it as a technique motorcyclists use in order to wake themselves up a bit if they feel drowsy. It began happening with some regularity so finally I asked him, "What's going on here?" And he said, "I'm feeling sleepy so that's what I have to do." Then he started this odd ritual where we would come into our scheduled hotel in the afternoon and he would go straight to bed, close his eyes, and lay there with his hands folded. That would be the end of the day for him. Often, I would go off to get some dinner by myself. In the mornings, I would be faced with this grumpy guy who was becoming increasingly recalcitrant. He didn't want to participate in anything. It was just like constantly dragging a bowling ball behind you. That's when I started thinking, "Maybe this head injury is more of a problem than I realized."

The next time he started doing the back and forth weaving it became even more dangerous. He was standing up on the bike and stretching out, waving his arms and exhibiting risky and irresponsible behavior. Finally, I went to Werner and said, "You know something's not right with Geoff. He claims that he's sleeping okay, but he's drowsy all day on the bike and I think that's he's an accident waiting to happen." Werner agreed that Geoff's behavior could pose a big problem, not just for the immediate tour, but it could also cause long range insurance complications for Edelweiss. "What do you want me to do?" he asked. I answered without a moment's hesitation. "Werner, I want to take the bike away from him and I want you to back me up." We both knew that would be hard on Geoff, but it was the wisest course of action.

On every Edelweiss Tour, there were sweep trucks and vans that carried luggage and spare bikes. We decided Geoff's bike could go on the sweep truck and he could travel in one of the vans. Werner and I took him aside and said, "Geoff, sorry, but you're a hazard to yourself and others and we can't have that." Geoff didn't like being told that he wasn't capable and tried to argue with us, but Werner and I stood firm. He was put in the front seat of a van which my buddy from Chicago, Burt Richmond, happened to be driving. According to Burt, Geoff sat in the corner of the front seat and fumed the whole time.

After that tour Geoff became so intractable that I finally started thinking, "What am I doing here and why am I was doing any of this?" Eventually, it got to the point where I no longer could deny what his every action was clearly saying – "I don't want to do this anymore. I don't want to go touring around the world on a motorcycle and I don't want to leave Australia." He was trying to tell me something I didn't want to hear. For me, the joy of touring and exploring on a motorcycle was still central to my life; it kept me feeling alive and vital. Without that singular joy in my life, I didn't know what I would do or who I would become.

We did go on one more tour together, to Spain, in 1995 – it would be our last. The tour included some spectacular art and architecture – two of my favorite subjects. But everywhere we went, Geoff had no interest in seeing what Spain had to offer. One day a busload of us went to a house outside of Barcelona that had been turned into a beautiful museum. When we got there, Geoff decided to stay in the bus; he was being very uncooperative and it became like having a stubborn toddler with you, "I'm not going to go anywhere. I want my candy!" On that day, I decided it was best to just let him be. He could stay in the bus and I would go on the museum tour with the rest of the group.

At some point, Burt Richmond and I came out of the museum and in a friendly gesture he may have put his arm around me or taken hold of my hand. It was no big deal. But obviously, Geoff was keeping an eye on us.

When we got back on the bus, he practically had steam coming out of his ears and was ready to choke Burt. "Don't you touch my girl!" he hissed. Burt was very diplomatic and said, "Listen Geoff, that will never happen again." I don't think I said a word. I was in shock. I tried to figure out where this was coming from, but my best guess was that Geoff was harboring ill feeling towards Burt ever since he was put in the van with him on the South Africa trip. Then again, maybe it was because he sensed we were two Americans who already had a natural affinity for each other. Whatever his reason, it exposed that unattractive, possessive side of Geoff that I had been willing to overlook or attribute to the accident. Now I was beginning to see it as a true personality trait that wasn't going away – one that I found increasingly difficult to tolerate.

The following year, Burt Richmond was doing another Lotus Tour of Spain. Because of Geoff's unseemly behavior on the previous trip, I felt as if I'd missed out on all that Spain had to offer. I was eager to go on the trip and I mentioned it to Geoff. The conversation became heated, and he told me in no uncertain terms that he was done with motorcycling and touring and in fact made it quite clear that he didn't ever want to go to America again. That was all I needed to make my decision. I would do the Spain trip with Burt and his group on my own.

This time Spain was delightful. Burt didn't have his wife with him (they had divorced) and I didn't have Geoff, so we just hung out together as buddies. Burt was willing to listen to all my fears and hopes for the future and I was willing to listen to his. One night over dinner, Burt told me about a Peking to Paris car rally that he had signed up for five years earlier and how at the last minute the geopolitical situation had gotten so nasty, that it got cancelled. The rally promised to be a thrilling adventure through a challenging foreign terrain where very few Westerners had ever been. In addition, it held the glamour of receiving world-wide attention because it marked the 90th anniversary of the original Peking to Paris rally of 1907. At the finish line in Paris, prize winners in several categories would be celebrated. It sounded truly exciting, and I told Burt that I hoped they could get it up and running again so that he would be able to take part in something so historically significant.

The Spain trip worked out very well and several months later, I joined Burt and his group on a tour to India. Again, Geoff chose to stay home. I had become close friends with all the guys on Burt's Lotus Tours and they knew about me and Geoff and what we were going through. One night we all got to talking and I finally opened up to them and said, "What am I going to do guys? I love this guy but I'm miserable and it's just not fun anymore." For the most part, they just shook their heads – they had no answers for me. That's when Burt casually piped in, "You remember that Peking to Paris rally I told you about? It's back on." That got my attention. "Really? And you're driving in it?" Burt nodded, "Yeah, along with my buddy, Rich Newman. We're co-driving a 1953 Citroen Deux Chevaux." "Wow! That sounds fantastic – lucky you!" Burt cocked his head sideways, gave me a smile and said, "You want to have some fun? Why don't you meet us along the way? You could come to Beijing for the start of the rally, then you could meet up with us in Katmandu, because that's going to be a two-nighter, then meet us again in Istanbul for another overnighter and then you could show up at the finish line in Paris." I looked at him and said, "Burt, really? You want me to be your cheerleader? No. I want to do the trip. You know, with a car!" The words came out of my mouth before I even had a chance to think about what I was saying. Burt didn't question me for a second. He immediately picked up the phone and called Phillip Young, the organizer of the Peking to Paris Rally.

"Phil, I've got this American gal here. She wants to sign up. I know it's late; what do you think?"

My heart was pounding with excitement as I watched Burt cradle the phone and mutter unintelligible things like, "Mmm," "Oh, yeah," "Sure. I understand." It didn't sound hopeful and I was dying to know the other side of the conversation. When Burt hung up he paused for a long moment, shook his head, looked at me with a crooked smile and said, "Get out your checkbook, Linda. You're in."

Just like that, the next part of my life began, and I knew in no uncertain terms that I would now have to deal with something I had been avoiding for a long time.

～ひ

BREAKING UP WITH GEOFF was one of the hardest things I ever had to do but I didn't want to drag it out. My thinking was, it's like pulling a bandage off a wound – better to do it quickly. I steeled myself for what was to come and as soon as I returned from India I sat down with Geoff for a serious talk. I told him I had come to a decision and no longer wanted us to be a couple. I assured him we could remain friends and I would always care about him, but our lives were going in very different directions and we needed to acknowledge that. I told him I was going back to America the following day to prepare for the Peking to Paris Rally. I would be back in four months, which would give him enough time to think about what his next move would be. Needless to say, Geoff was caught off guard, with no ready response. Whatever else there was to say was left hanging in the air.

The next morning as I stepped on the plane for San Francisco, I felt confident I had l made the right decision. For six years I had struggled in the hopes that the magical romance Geoff and I once had enjoyed would someday return. But finally, I had accepted the truth; my fantasy of "happily-ever-after" was never going to be. As the plane lifted off the tarmac and Oz fell away below me, the enormity of what I had just done, not only to myself but to Geoff, struck me full force. I began to cry. Not soft rolling tears, but wracking sobs that brought the airline stewardess to my side. Concerned about my well-being she knelt beside me, put her arms around me and let me pour out all my pent-up pain. She comforted me for hours, until I calmed down and could face the fact that I had just severed the most tender part of my heart and left it with a broken man, living alone in the suburbs of Melbourne.

CHAPTER 21

Prepping for Peking

March – October 1997

The Peking to Paris Rally was coming up quickly and I was under a lot of pressure to start planning for it. Not only did I need to secure a car, but I needed to find a co-driver. As I quickly learned, rally cars were generally driven by teams of two people who switched off as driver and navigator. Burt had already decided it would be great for me to drive a Jeep. "An American girl in an American Jeep. What an amazing symbol that would be!" Philip Young shot that down fast, "No Burt, no four-wheeled vehicles allowed. But I do have this 1968 Hillman Hunter that your friend could purchase." The Hillman was a boxy family car, sort of a British version of a Dodge Dart, with four doors and an automatic transmission plus an overdrive fifth gear. I had never driven a Hillman but that was no problem. I had never participated in a car rally either, so it was all new to me. Learning something new was comforting to me so I was up for anything. I said, "Sure, let's do that. Sign me up."

My next challenge was to find a co-driver who could handle what was going to be a grueling trip. Burt knew a girl in San Francisco named Karen Masden, who owned a couple of three-wheeled BMW vehicles and had more knowledge about cars than I did. I thought that was a good start. She and I met up and she seemed okay, so I started making a schedule of all the things we had to take care of: Paperwork, vaccinations, camping gear. I laid it all out for Karen and quickly sensed she was kind of flighty and wasn't going to hold up her end. I thought, "A friend of a friend is nice, but she's not showing me that she's a great team player." That meant I would end up being far too responsible for everything, which made me nervous. I informed Karen it wasn't going to work out and let her go. Now I was back to square one with no idea of how to find a reliable co-driver. I knew there must be someone out there who would be perfect and I just had to keep my eyes and ears open and have faith we would find each other.

A few nights later, I roared into a gas station on my bike and spotted a car decorated with automotive emblems. Surrounding it was a group of guys who were obviously rally drivers. I pulled off my helmet and sauntered in their direction. I could see they were sizing me up and quickly decided I was OK. They were extremely friendly so I came right out with what was on mind. "I wonder if you guys might be able to help me out. I'm looking for a female co-driver to do the Peking to Paris rally." They reacted like I was crazy, but once I convinced them I was doing the rally they became truly interested. One of them suggested I contact Martin Swig, a very well-known older gentleman in San Francisco whose name I recognized from the newspapers. He was from a wealthy family and owned a classic car collection. One of the rally guys gave me his phone number with the assurance, "He knows everybody in the auto world." I called him the very next day.

He was extremely enthusiastic about my request and said, "I'd love to come over to your place. We'll sit down and talk about it." I figured he rightfully wanted to check me out before he would extend himself on my behalf. He showed up at my place on a Sunday afternoon and I gave him a brief rundown on what I had been doing for the past ten years – learning to ride a motorcycle, going to Australia, my solo crossing to Perth as both a guide and a passenger on multiple bike tours. He was impressed.

"Linda, most people who have your wherewithal wouldn't even bother to put themselves out there. I applaud your courage."

I thanked him for his praise but stressed that what I really needed was to find a co-driver. Without hesitation he said, "Genevieve Obert. You've got to meet Gennie Obert. She's an automotive writer, lives in Santa Cruz with her husband and kids. They run a Fiat parts warehouse and they're familiar with car rallies in Europe. I think this would be right up her alley. I'll give you her phone number." I breathed a sigh of relief. It looked like my faith was about to be rewarded.

I contacted Genevieve Obert right away and asked if she would be interested in being my co-driver on the Peking to Paris Rally. I explained I would be fronting all the costs of the trip and she would be responsible for sharing the driving and navigating duties. Her answer? "Hell yes, I'd love to do it." My heart leapt with joy! It was exactly the enthusiastic response I was looking for. "So why don't we meet up?" she went on. "My mom and I will come up to see you in San Francisco and we'll hang out and talk about how to get this thing going." I quickly got a sense that she was rooting for her mother to be included as a passenger in the back seat. There was no way I was going to be responsible for another person, let alone one who was coming along just for the ride. I let her talk for about ten minutes while my mind raced, trying to decide if this was going to be a deal breaker. Finally, I just came out with it and said, "No, we're not carrying any extra passengers. We're going to need every square inch for our supplies." Without any argument Gennie agreed it should just be the two of us. That was a relief. It made me feel I could be straight with her and she would be easy to work with. Now I could concentrate on the enormous task of preparing for the rally.

Besides the practical challenges of assembling all the necessary emergency car parts and personal items for the trip, there was a lot to learn about the rules and regulations of the rally itself. I never realized how much the rest of the world was caught up in car rallies. South America, Africa, Europe, Great Britain – there's always some sort of rally going on, even if it's just a weekend event. It's a fun group thing where people can get out, get their old cars on the road and enjoy a nice meal and drinks at the end of the day. The real excitement comes from being challenged by the clock. In the Peking to Paris Rally we would be racing against our own clocks. The rules required every driver to leave at a certain time of day and arrive at one or two predetermined rally stops along the way, also at specific times.

There would be monitors at the check points who would mark your time on a card; then off you'd go again. If you showed up late or early, you'd get demerit points. At the end of the day, you had to arrive at your hotel at exactly the time you'd been given for that day. Assignments would be given the night before and it would say something like, "Show up at the start, ready to go at 6:41 a.m." Each car would be sent out one minute behind the other so you were really racing against yourself and it was the navigator's job to keep the driver adhering to the clock. The big reward at the end of that 10,000-mile trip was a trophy for the team that crossed the finish line first. There were also various ribbons for other achievements depending on how few demerits you had accumulated. There was a gold medal, a silver medal, and a bronze medal. I knew I would be happy if we came home with any of those prizes.

Shortly before we left for Beijing, I received word from Geoff that he had moved into his parents' unit in Adelaide, over four hundred miles north-west of Melbourne. His parents were both living in a retirement home and their place was now standing empty. Certainly, from Geoff's point of view, it was a smart thing to do. The unit was completely paid for and there was nothing to keep him in Melbourne anymore. But for me it was a hard blow. Even though we were no longer a couple, I remained closely connected to Geoff and wanted the comfort of knowing he was somewhere safe. Worst of all, his messages contained hints of suicidal thinking – "I'll probably go out into the desert and crawl inside an empty log where no one will ever find me." I didn't know if Geoff was being melodramatic or if he was in a seriously depressed state of mind, but I was determined that when I got back I would try to find a way to get him some help.

⁓

THE FIRST TIME GENNIE AND I saw our red Hillman Hunter was on a quick weekend trip we made to the UK along with her husband, Chris, who came with us to check the car's mechanicals. My first impression of the Hillman was that it was not much to look at. A plain family car, hardly noteworthy and not at all the romantic image of what a contender in such a prestigious race should look like. The only notable thing that set it apart was its red color. Gennie's husband was satisfied with the car's condition and she and I each got to test drive it with Phillip Young in the passenger seat to assess our driving abilities. Gennie was familiar with rallies and her test drive went well. In my case — not so good. The only rally experience I'd had was one lesson I'd taken in San Francisco. Phillip was shocked at my lack of skills and didn't hide his concern. That only made me more determined to show him how successful and how skillful I could be. I was sure that whatever rally skills were needed, I would acquire along the way.

When we arrived in Beijing we got right to work. The cars had been shipped in from all over the world and we drivers had to get them out of storage, set them up and check them out. When we managed to find the Hillman amongst the sea of cars in a covered warehouse, with the official number "51" boldly painted on her sides making her mundane profile appear somewhat elevated, I thought, "Yes, this little red car can do it!"

On our second day in Beijing, Phillip Young came by to inform us that there were three teams from Iran coming to join the rally and they were all driving Hillman Paykans. The Paykan was the same car as our Hillman Hunter, only manufactured in Tehran. That meant we could become part of a Hunter/Paykan team. Phillip advised us that it would be a good idea to join forces with the Iranians, "When you have multiples of the same cars, you can help each other. You might even have spare parts that you can swap around." Gennie and I looked at each other and thought, "Wow, two American women and six Iranian guys?" That sounded like a good team to us!

Once we had our cars set up, the drivers all gathered to attend meetings where we were given instructions and maps. It was also a chance for us to meet our fellow drivers. Phillip Young had managed to pull together a field of almost one hundred cars — everything from classic Bentleys and Rolls Royces to our unassuming Hillman and Burt Richmond's even more modest 1953 Citroën Deux Chevaux (a French equivalent of a Volkswagen). What we also learned early on was that despite a handful of professional drivers, very few of the almost two hundred participants had ever rallied before. Most, like me, were adventurous types who wanted to be part of something historic and could afford the steep entry price.

It was getting close to rally day and Gennie and I kept looking around wondering, "Where are those Iranian fellas?" Then one evening, we were waiting for the hotel elevator and when the doors opened there stood six handsome, tall, Middle Eastern looking guys. Gorgeous? Oh my God! Really good for the eyeballs! I don't know what possessed me, but I walked into the elevator and said, "So who are you? The Iranians?" Mr. Handsome, who had the best English, grabbed me by my shoulders and said, "Why, do we look like terrorists?" Instantly the ice was broken and we became buddies and teammates.

One of the reasons I was eager to do the Peking to Paris Rally was because my curiosity about the rest of the world was insatiable and this rally offered an opportunity to visit places I would not otherwise have been able to see. Parts of China were forbidden to Westerners and Americans weren't allowed to enter Iran. For the Paykan teams, this was the first time they had been allowed to leave Iran. They were all professional drivers but had only participated in rallies in their home country. I'll never know how Phillip Young managed to get around all those political issues, but he did.

On the morning of September 6, 1997, the Second Peking to Paris Motor Challenge got underway. With much fanfare, we took off from the Great Wall of China surrounded by a crowd of traditionally costumed well-wishers who lined the road for miles and cheered enthusiastically as we rolled by. We were all eager to get out onto the open road, but the throng of admiring fans continued to line the route for the next four days and we were forced to drive in a slow-moving convoy with a police escort in order to avoid hitting bystanders who crowded close to our cars and reached out to touch us. Thankfully, when we finally made it to Inner Mongolia, the crowds subsided, but the paved highway also disappeared. It was the beginning of the ever-deteriorating road conditions.

Gennie and I decided early on that we would switch off every other day between the driving and navigating. Gennie had really good driving skills and was easy to get along with. Her biggest problem was her height. She was a very tall girl, about 6' 3", gangly and not very robust. The kind of girl who was so tall in fifth grade, you know she tried to shrink herself. Gennie found the Hillman extremely uncomfortable and when it was her turn to drive she spent all kinds of time trying to push the seat back. There was nowhere for it to go. We had removed the back seat and jammed the empty space full of supplies including bottled water, snacks, and a vast array of tools and auto parts. Not only was the Hillman a short car but Gennie had super long legs. She was constantly trying to get her hips freed up from being jammed into her pelvis. I knew she was having a tough time, but compared to the jolting and jarring we were both experiencing from the almost non-existent road, her hip discomfort was a secondary problem.

Everywhere along our route, we encountered broken-down vehicles, carts, and wagons that had been left where they died. The deeply rutted roads began to take a serious toll on some of the cars including a Rolls Royce that met up with a mud-covered water buffalo which sliced through the chassis, rendering it undriveable. Any notions that this was going to be a pleasant ride through the Asian continent were quickly dispelled.

CHAPTER 22

Iran - Paris

October 1997

Somewhere between Tibet and Katmandu we met up with our own minor disaster. I was driving and we were on a dusty road. The only Porsche in the rally sped past us and stirred up a huge cloud of dust. I couldn't see a thing and ended up driving off the side of the road into a culvert. Unlike the round culverts in America, this was just kind of a rock slab. I hit that slab with the right front tire and it came up through the floor board, right between Gennie's ankles.

Once the dust settled and we realized we'd had what they call in Australia "a prang," we checked each other to see if we'd been hurt – luckily, we hadn't. Then, seemingly out of nowhere, all these wiry Tibetan men, women, and children appeared. Gennie and I were down in this culvert; I'm a 5'5" petite blond woman in rally gear and heavy driving boots and Gennie is dark and 6'3". We were not what these native Tibetans saw every day. Gennie began uncurling herself from the car, getting taller by the second. The Tibetans were on the road above looking down at us like we were Martians. Everybody was gesturing and jabbering and of course we couldn't understand a word. But without any way to communicate with us, they decided to get the car up on the road. They surrounded the vehicle, which was loaded with all our stuff, and started this sort of "heave-ho" Tibetan chant in order to get everybody in synch. Their skinny arms were all muscle and in no time, they had picked up the car and put it up on the road. Gennie and I were gob smacked! We'd never seen anything like that.

The Hillman wasn't drivable, but at least it was up on the road. To their credit, the Rally organizers had arranged for three teams of mechanics in Land Rovers who could come to your aid for anything that could be fixed in under fifteen minutes. If the repair took more time than that, you were on your own. As luck would have it, one of the Land Rover teams showed up rather quickly. Gennie spoke the language of cars and could talk in terms the guys would understand. For the most part, we were able to handle our own repairs and never went looking for help. We weren't damsels in distress, but it always was appreciated when these angels showed up. As it turned out, our controlling arm and heavy cross bar had been bent into a "U" shape. They set their timer and started banging away. With the help of a vise, which they carried in their Land Rover, they were able to straighten it out enough for us to proceed. The car was a bit wobbly and we would have to get further repairs that night at our encampment, but we were able to make our time without demerits. The whole culvert episode took about an hour and half which put us perilously close to falling behind our sole competitors for the All-Female Team medal, two British women driving a Volvo Amazon. Gennie and I were determined to take home that prize.

THE NEXT LEG OF THE JOURNEY took us through some of the most treacherous terrain imaginable. We were leaving the Himalayas heading towards Nepal on a road that cut back and forth along sheer rock cliffs where waterfalls came rushing at us intermittently and rocks bounced down the face of the cliffs as if shaken loose by our very presence. One large boulder landed directly in front of one of the cars, missing it by inches. It was like a scenario out of a nail-biting Hollywood movie. All the time, the red Hillman was struggling with weakened steering.

By the time we arrived in Katmandu, the mechanic who built our car had flown in from London with tools and spare parts he brought with him on the plane. With the aid of a group of Nepalese mechanics, he spent the entire day making the needed repairs. Gennie and I thought it would be a good time to clean out the sand and grit that had seeped in to all our supplies. We had barely gotten underway when we realized that all around us the Nepalese mechanics were lighting up acetylene torches without using face shields and working perilously close to the growing puddles of fuel that were leaking from damaged cars. The danger of an imminent explosion made us rethink our desire for cleanliness and we got out of there fast. Our repairs were made without further calamity and the Hillman, though it would never be good as new, was ready to take on the rest of the race.

~~~

THE ENTIRE RALLY LASTED forty-three days. Fourteen of them were spent in China and would turn out to be the most difficult part of the whole trip. China is vast with long stretches of undeveloped terrain. Many of our nights were spent camping out in tents, sometimes in weather so freezing cold that we crawled into our sleeping bags with our wet clothes on. Villages were few and far between, but every time we came into a village the people would be lining the streets in their unique beautiful Tibetan garb. The streets would be decorated with banners and all kinds of symbols wishing us good luck. I felt badly for them because they were expecting us to stop, to have a feast and enjoy their hospitality. We'd slow down and wave, but we wouldn't stay; we just kept going. I thought, "That's a terrible thing to do to innocent people who've made such a big deal out of our arrival."

That wasn't the only thing that disturbed me about the rally. There were times when we were a real hazard to the local population. While the word "rally" may sound impressive, when you're in a Third World country, you rarely ever get above thirty miles an hour. Still, that's a lot faster than most of the locals drive. There were pedestrians around who really had no sense of the danger of cars going that fast and I couldn't help but feel that we were part of an accident waiting to happen. Broken down trucks were a common sight in China, but one day we came across a truck that was pulled over to the side of the road and next to it an injured Chinese man was lying on the ground. From what I could gather when the rally cars came whizzing by, this guy stepped out from behind his truck to see what was going on and two German drivers in a 1930s Mercedes clipped him. We all stopped and tried to help. I knew from my nursing experience that he had a head injury because one of his eyes was completely dilated. Very quickly a police car arrived and the police took charge of the scene. The story we were told that night was that the man had a broken arm, which I knew was not true. That started my disillusionment with how our "fun excursion" was potentially endangering the locals. I may not have been aware of that fact before the rally, but the trip organizers knew; they were prepared with something like a dozen body bags just in case there were wrecks or deaths from hypothermia.

I was glad to leave Nepal, even though crossing into India was the most entangled political mess imaginable. It took hours of sorting through endless red tape to finally allow us to cross the border. The worst was yet to come. In India, we lost our horn for a day. That may not sound like such a big deal, but in India your car horn is the most essential tool for navigating their unspeakably awful traffic. Side or rearview mirrors are not common safety equipment and are rarely installed on most trucks, vans, carts, camels, cows, or goats (all of which are found on their crowded roads). It's the job of the rear approaching vehicle to warn from behind by blowing their horn indicating that they want to pass and then waiting for the OK gesture from the guy in front in order to make their move. Without a horn, we were obviously at a terrible disadvantage. It was a miracle we made it through India without an automotive disaster.

IN INDIA AND PAKISTAN, the roads became noticeably better, but the driving conditions were far more dangerous. Beside the unimaginable heat and vast miles of endless desert terrain, we encountered a roadblock consisting of one young soldier complete with a very large rifle hanging from his shoulder. Gennie was driving this day and as we approached the soldier, he began pulling up a wire as a signal to stop. I made it very clear to Gennie the one thing we were not going to do was stop! I told her to drive right through the wire if she had to. Gratefully, the young soldier dropped the wire to the ground just as we approached him. It wasn't until some years later that it dawned on me that we were at the mercy of an Al Qaeda guard and that our next stop, Quetta, Pakistan, was the headquarters of that terrorist group.

The next thing I remember is seeing all of these Biblical towns fashioned out of sand, ancient looking but with satellite dishes on the roofs of huts. It was the kind of cultural juxtaposition that was hard to get your head around.

THE RALLY ORGANIZERS PROMISED us was that we'd never be driving in the dark. Well, so much for that promise. On the last day in Pakistan, we got caught in some sort of a climb up this hillside mountain in bumper-to-bumper traffic due to a tipped overloaded truck, which I had earlier dubbed "dead elephants." It was getting late and we were getting tired. Nobody uses headlights. So we were faced with traffic coming toward us that we couldn't see until our headlights hit their trucks, which in India and Pakistan are all covered with reflectors. Nothing prepared us for the shock of hundreds of explosions of circles of red, white, and gold that almost blinded us. And these Indian drivers thought it was a game to run us off the road. There were no streetlights and because we couldn't see, we didn't know when we were going to end up in another culvert.

In one day, the rally suffered over a dozen accidents, including the tragic deaths of a German father and son team, Joseph and Rene Feit, who lost control of their VW convertible and dove underneath a stalled Pakistani bus. The son, Rene, was killed instantly, and his father died five hours later on his fiftieth birthday. It was such a tragic waste of two beautiful lives and I was flabbergasted because the powers that be didn't seem to be fazed by it. Their attitude was just very business-like, "You take a risk and things like that happen."

In sharp contrast to India was our arrival in Iran where the roads were good (white painted lines down the middle and on the sides) and the Iranians went all out to welcome us in style, especially our Iranian teammates the Hunter/Paykan drivers. We were escorted all seven days in Iran by the Car Club of Iran. By now Gennie and I had become great friends with the six handsome guys, even more so after we were able to help them with exactly the spare parts they needed when their cars broke down. On their home turf, they were like sports heroes. In the town of Isfahan, which was about mid-way through the trip, they took us to meet their wives, kids, parents, brothers, sisters, some of whom had studied in America. They very quietly made it known to us that once they were in their homes the strict religious practices that governed all their public behavior would be left at the front door. The veils would come off and they would find ways to drink, dance and listen to popular music – all forbidden pleasures. It was part of a schizophrenic lifestyle that many Iranians had been forced to adopt. One of the rally drivers witnessed a woman being chastised on the street for improper clothing and then whisked away in a police car.

One afternoon, I arrived at a mid-day time check only to have one of the Car Club members rush up to warn me to quickly adjust my now fallen scarf before any of the officials saw me. Full body covering was required for the seven days in Iran, and Gennie and I never adjusted to wearing a heads-carf while driving. It wouldn't be until the Iran/Turkey border that we would be able to shed the various voluminous pieces of clothing it took to pass the "cover the female body head to toe" police. The relief was palpable among all of the rally participants.

In Tabriz, Iran, as everywhere, people along the way were excited to see us. Whenever they saw the red Hillman (probably the only one in the whole country) and spotted the two women drivers, their reaction was always great surprise followed by enthusiastic cheering. As we were leaving one Turkish town, a long line of schoolgirls in their white scarves lined up just to wave goodbye. I loved seeing the broad smiles on their faces. Again, I felt we were showing these young provincial girls that women could do exciting and daring things. Whether it would have any effect on their lives, we'd never know.

By the time we left Iran and headed for Turkey, I was ready for this rally to be over. We needed new tires and a replacement windshield wiper motor. Istanbul was a two-day layover, but we spent the better part of one of those days slowly crawling through the most traffic jammed city I had ever experienced. What a nightmare! All I could think about was our arrival in Paris. I called it "smelling the barn." Eager as I was for it to end, we still had many miles to go.

We crossed from Turkey into Greece with the dormant volcano of Mount Ararat dominating the horizon. After two quick days driving through Greece, we loaded onto a giant Mediterranean ship for an over-night trip from Patras, Greece, to Rimini, on the East Coast of Italy. It was one of the areas of Italy I'd never been to and it reminded me of the beach towns in California. That was the enjoyable part of Italy. Soon after, Gennie and I came very close to losing our lives on one of those notorious twisty Italian roads in the Dolomites and Alps. Italian drivers are known to take those roads at ridiculous speeds and a guy came at us around a particularly treacherous bend head on, so close that we both thought it was the end. After that we were anxious to get the rally over with.

Our next leg was a drive through Austria and into Germany, with snow and ice to add excitement. By now we were visiting places I'd already been on my bike and there wasn't much new or interesting. I did get to meet up briefly with my motorcycle friends from Edelweiss Touring which was fun, but then shortly after, we drove through the village of the father and son who had been killed in Pakistan. Black bands were tied on all our cars and we took a very slow procession through the town. The family and all the townspeople were lined up to pay tribute to the two men they had lost. As we passed the line of their family members, I couldn't help but think how painful it must have been to have had their loved ones shipped back in body bags and to see the remnants of the convertible VW Bug. It was another reason for me to think, "Why do people do this?"

Considering how many people were in this crazy event and how many dangers we faced, we were lucky there were only two casualties. When we hit France and were heading into Paris I said to Gennie, "I know it's your turn to drive, but I'm going to pull rank and insist I drive up to the finish line." We both knew all along I would be the one driving across the finish line. Gennie had no problem with that. I had sponsored the whole endeavor. She was a truly gracious and grateful woman and recognized that there was no way she could ever have afforded this trip on her own. She'd had a blast; she loved it. For me, she'd been an invaluable partner and I was proud to share the trip with her. But when it came to the finish line, that's where I wanted my moment in the sun.

On October 18, 1997, a beautiful sunny Saturday, we entered Paris. By that time the Hillman was limping on its last legs. Our clutch was almost gone and the only way to get it into gear was to stop the car entirely and then shift into first and carry on until the next time we had to downshift. But we were as determined as the other eighty-five cars that crossed the finish line. Of that number, only sixty-six had qualified for any kind of medal and we would all soon learn who the winners were based on our accumulated scores.

The streets of Paris were filled with people celebrating our arrival. In that miraculous moment of crossing the finish line after having driven 10,000 miles, I jumped out of my car and shouted to the world "Yay! We did it!"

Neither Gennie nor I had any family or friends to greet us, but we did have one supporter. He was David Steele, a Parliamentarian who was to have been a participant in the race driving another Hillman Hunter, but had dropped out when he was granted a Lordship by the Queen herself. David was there to congratulate us and wanted to know how the race had gone. All I could say was, "You missed out on a good ride."

The overall Rally winners were John Bayliss and Phil Surtees who won in a 1942 Ford Jeep (even though I had been told no four-wheeled vehicles were allowed!). When the rest of the medals were announced, Gennie and I managed to grab the Gold, coming in with under twenty minutes of accumulated demerits over the 10,000 miles. In addition, we also won The Women's Cup. It was a thrill of a lifetime, but like all challenges it came with mixed emotions and left me wondering if it was all worth it. The cost of two drivers who died in an accident and other victims of the race who happened to be at the wrong place at the wrong time – just standing by the side of the road! It was in that frame of mind that I returned to San Francisco, ready to take on the problems I knew Geoff was facing. I couldn't get out of Paris fast enough.

CHAPTER 23

Last Gasp

1997-2000

I returned from the Peking to Paris Rally in late October 1997 and immediately turned my attention to Geoff. Because of the horrific faxes he had been sending, I knew his mental condition was unstable and I told my travel agent to get him a ticket to San Francisco from Melbourne as soon as possible. Even though Geoff no longer wanted to travel outside of Australia, I managed to convince him that I was going to be able to help him. He agreed to come to San Francisco, but only for a short stay. A counselor I had used previously recommended a psychiatrist and I made an appointment for Geoff to see him. Besides his loss of taste and smell, Geoff had short term memory problems that scared the hell out of him. The day after he arrived, we sat down with the psychiatrist, who after examining Geoff, gave us a hopeful prognosis, "I really think you're depressed and I think your memory will come back if we can get on top of this depression." He recommended one of those highly touted anti-depression serotonin drugs. "It will take a couple of weeks for it to show significant results, but hang in there. I think this will finally help turn some things around for you." It was a tremendous relief to hear there was a possible solution. Unfortunately, because Geoff wasn't his patient, he could only advise him as to what he thought he should be taking. Geoff would have to go back to his doctor in Australia and get a prescription there. Geoff was eager to get started with the medication and within a few days he left.

I was feeling optimistic after having found him a promising solution until I started getting the faxes of how problematic it was to obtain the medication. Because Australia has socialized medicine, they had all kinds of rules and regulations governing this type of drug. It wasn't part of the diagnostic protocol in Australia and they were refusing to give it to him. I could sense Geoff was becoming extremely angry and unstable. I remember showing his fax to the San Francisco doctor and attempting to convey the urgency, "This is part of the problem; he's not able to get this stuff." The doctor was sympathetic and I think we were getting ready to smuggle some to him when I got another fax from Geoff. As it turned out, Geoff had become so enraged that he threatened his doctor and finally wore him down. The doctor made him sign a release form absolving him of all responsibility and Geoff finally got his prescription. In three days, he woke up and was his old self. Even at a long distance I could tell it was a profound change and in the long run it helped re-establish our friendship and gave me a reason to think about going back to Australia.

Over the next few months, we kept in touch with emails and phone calls, which is how I learned Geoff had sold his parents' retirement unit in Adelaide and used the money to buy this very old, very interesting pioneer-type house in Birdwood, South Australia. He described it as this cute "wattle and daub,"— the term they use for a house that's been built with mud and branches. The "wattle" is made up of branches of whatever vegetation is native to the area and the "daub" is the mud they use to help strengthen it and give it bonding. They slather it up onto beams and boards and around the doorways and windows — much like an adobe house. I had been to Birdwood many times on our Mulga tours. I liked the town a lot, plus my passion and curiosity about architecture and renovation kicked in and I was eager to see Geoff's new place. At some point I asked, "Would you mind if I came over to see what you've done?" He said, "Yeah, sure. I'd love to have you come by." Despite all we'd gone through, we both knew we were still deeply connected.

ONCE AGAIN, I FOUND myself excited to be flying into Melbourne. I still had my house on Canning Street, where I hung out for a day or two to say "Hi," to all my friends; then I got in my car and drove the eight hours from Melbourne, Victoria, to Birdwood, South Australia. It was great to see the change in Geoff that the medication had brought about and to experience the unusual architecture of the wattle and daub house. It was on the crude side, but pretty efficient; naturally cool in the summer and warm in the winter with a cozy fireplace. It was a kooky, funny house that I instantly fell in love with. Somehow that gave us a reason to be good friends again. I really enjoyed that, because selfishly, I also wanted an excuse to be able to keep coming back to Australia.

It felt comfortable being back with Geoff and right away I helped him figure out how to best use the rooms for modern day living. Our relationship had taken on a whole new dimension, almost like a brother and sister. Even though we slept in the same bed, sex was out of the question. It had been for quite a while, so that wasn't an issue. We were really enjoying each other's company, when darn if the place next door didn't come up for sale. It wasn't anything as unique as Geoff's wattle and daub place, but it was a decent "salt box" structure. My first thought was, "I could do something nice with that," and my second thought was, "I'm going to buy it!"

I didn't rush into it. Geoff didn't try to talk me out of it and by the time I got back to San Francisco I knew I wanted that house and I bought it over the internet. It was probably the first time anyone had ever bought a house in Australia on the internet. Certainly not in Birdwood. My first order of business was to renovate. Naturally, I called on architect Michael Rigg who had done such a great job on my Canning Street house in Melbourne. Again, working together, we were able to turn that little "Ned Kelly" salt box house into something special.

Living next door to Geoff became a perfect solution for two people who really liked each other, who had been though a lot together and still had enough in common that they wanted to hang on to their friendship. He'd come over to my place for dinner and to watch our favorite TV shows and I'd go over to his place for breakfast. It was a great platonic relationship, but

I was craving a bit more intimacy. In fact, at one point, I said to him, "You know, we could be friends with benefits." He was mortified, shocked that a woman would ask to have friend sex. It didn't suit his sense of morality and made me realize that if I was going to find any kind of physical fulfillment, I would have to look elsewhere.

For the next couple of years, I maintained that bi-hemispheric life, flying back and forth during the summers and avoiding the winters. Each time I returned, it seemed as if Geoff had been just moping around waiting for my return. The only thing that kept him busy or interested was working on cars or fixing things. In Birdwood, there was a National Motor Museum that supplied vehicles for parades and other public events. I could only imagine how much use they would have for a good auto mechanic and how perfect Geoff's talents would be for them. It took some convincing, but he finally did as I suggested and went to meet with the folks at the Motor Museum. It all turned out for the best; they were eager to have him and he loved the work.

On my next trip to Oz, instead of going to Birdwood, I stayed in Melbourne at the Canning Street house. I was trying to figure out what it would be like to be a single woman in Australia. I had friends there, couples of course, but that wasn't any fun. After a few weeks I began thinking, "Hell it's hard enough to be single in the States. I don't want to be single in Australia." Besides, I was looking forward to being a grandma. Maida was about to get married to her boyfriend Willem and I always felt that having grandchildren was going to be part of my future. I could see a day coming when I'd take that last flight from Oz. So why would I try to fall in love with some other Aussie bloke? Once I came to that decision, things got a lot easier.

In 1999, I returned to San Francisco and threw myself into the planning of Maida's wedding. Maida and I agreed the best place to get married was in the wine country. One weekend we went driving around and after stopping at various places, we stumbled onto Beltane Ranch, a 105-acre Victorian farm and vineyard. Set in the middle was a historic inn surrounded by wide verandas and lush gardens. It was absolutely perfect. The inn had just enough rooms for the immediate wedding party. The wedding was set to take place in September, which meant there would be beautiful warm evenings and gorgeous sunsets. We both agreed this would be the spot. A week later Maida and I came back with Willem to get his approval.

We got a late start out of San Francisco and by the time we reached the wine country it was already lunch time. We decided we would stop at the next promising place to eat. A short way down the road I spotted a sign that pointed to the right and said, "Glen Ellen." Something drew me to it and I said, "Why don't we see where this road takes us?" Within a half a mile we came to a small town that looked as if it had been lifted out of Australia. There were small shops, an old saloon, and the kind of buildings you see all over Australia with second-floor verandas. It was this perfect duplicate town that had obviously been built around the same time as many of the Australian towns. It not only shared a similar historic timeline, but a lot of similar architecture and was very reminiscent of small Australian towns like Birdwood. We stopped and had a bite to eat and the whole time I couldn't stop thinking, "Wow, this is really something. This feels so comfortable to me." For the rest of the day that little town of Glen Ellen resonated with me.

JUST AS MAIDA AND I anticipated, Willem loved the Beltane Ranch and before the day was over the selection of the wedding site was a done deal. I hired my favorite caterer to do the party and luckily my ex-husband Larry said, "Do whatever you want and send me half the bill." Maida and I went to New York to have our dresses made. Geoff reluctantly came to the wedding as my escort. Of course, he had nothing appropriate to wear so I marched him out to a store in San Francisco and got him a nice suit. Even though he had agreed to take part in the festivities, Geoff was his same old grumpy self. Luckily, I had motorcycle friends from Utah at the wedding and Geoff knew them, so at least they could babysit him while I was busy being the mother of the bride – making speeches and dancing dances. It was great to be with all our family and friends, including the Schwabs, and by all accounts I had pulled off a gorgeous wedding.

The very next day I went back to Australia with Geoff for what would
be one of our last trips together. He was much happier at home and that's
where he wanted to stay. I already had one foot out the door and was looking around and thinking, "It's inevitable that there will be that last flight
from Australia." Perhaps, I thought, it could soften the blow if I could recreate Australia in California. I had been thinking a lot about Sonoma County
and Glen Ellen and immediately seized on the idea that somewhere in
Sonoma I could find my Australia. I had gathered many beautiful posses-
sions in Australia including custom furnishings and a fairly sizable Euro-
pean, Australian, and Indigenous art collection. Now what to do with it all
was solved. It would all be coming to California with me.

MELODY DUKE WAS the real estate agent who had helped me buy my
Culebra Terrace property in San Francisco in 1990. In addition, she was a
personal trainer who got me in shape for the Peking to Paris Rally. Over
the years we had become good friends and in the early Spring of 2000, I
called up Melody and said, "Come on, let's go find some places to look at
in Sonoma County." As usual, once I fixed my mind on an idea there was
no stopping me. Melody pulled together a list of properties and we began
our search. Once a week for almost eight weeks we made the fifty-mile
commute up Highway 101 to visit an amazing variety of homes, ranches,
farms, and vineyards. My criteria was that it had to be within an hour of
San Francisco and be on a road that wasn't too isolated so that when I was
alone, if there was an earthquake or a fire I could walk somewhere to get
help. Melody showed me some spectacular places with breathtaking views,
but they were up long winding roads. If you forgot to buy milk it was a long
haul back to the grocery store. I needed life and neighbors and the more we
looked, the more attractive the area surrounding the town of Glen Ellen
became. It had a certain liveliness that appealed to me. There were small
shops and markets and a sense of community. I liked that, and after looking
around for a while I decided we should concentrate on finding something
close to the town.

A couple of weeks later Melody took me to a place that was a mile from Glen Ellen. It was on Warm Springs Road, a charming, tree lined two-lane road that meandered through the gently rolling hills. The property was just off the main road up a short driveway. Melody had learned that the property included "three acres with a main house, two shacks, and another small house that sat on the edge of the Sonoma creek." From the moment we drove through the gate I knew we were on the right track. Majestic oak trees gave a magical feel to the place and even though the path to the creek was so overgrown you couldn't see it, I loved the fact that it was there.

We met up with the owner, Judy Thompson. Her father, George Thompson, had built the place ninety years ago and the family had lived there for generations. Judy's two sons had moved out of the area and had no interest in maintaining the property. She was eager to sell and lamented, "Nobody in the family wants it and frankly it's too much for me. I want to take my money and move to Oakmont Village, an adult community in Santa Rosa." Considering Judy's frame of mind, I felt I could get it at a reasonable price. I made a quick assessment that the place had great potential. It was going to be a major reconstruction job, but at this point in my life, I was ready to take on something big and exciting.

I had become a serial restorer for sure, ever since 1993, when I was bitten by the bug. I had already done more than a dozen rehabs, large and small, on two coasts and two hemispheres and over the years I experienced the satisfaction of putting a personal stamp on every one of those projects. Whenever I weighed making art in a rundown isolated studio against using those same muscles in a three-dimensional collaborative setting, the choice was obvious.

On our way back to San Francisco, we stopped at the Glen Ellen Village Market. I was delighted to discover a store so close by that was friendly and fun and well-stocked. That probably sealed the deal. Right away I thought, "This is it," and put in a bid. After a brief wait, in June of 2000, the old George Thompson property became mine. Now all I had to do was figure out how to deliver the spirit of Australia.

Major Geoff Coat, Retired, Royal Australian Army, 1991

The Great Ocean Road, Victoria, Australia, 1989

One Happy Motorcyclist, 1990

Introducing Geoff Coat to friends in San Francisco. Left to right, Me, Phil and Shari Lamanet, Karen Diefenbach, Mary Chomenko, and Geoff Coat, 1990

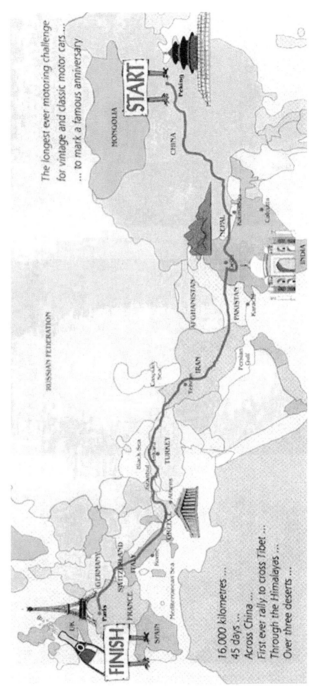

The longest ever motoring challenge for vintage and classic motor cars ...
... to mark a famous anniversary

16,000 kilometres ...
45 days ...
Across China ...
First ever rally to cross Tibet ...
Through the Himalayas ...
Over three deserts ...

Our Peking to Paris itinerary, 1997

Me on our humble little Hillman Hunter and Gennie Obert,
my co-driver for the Peking to Paris Rally, 1997

The Nepalese people welcome us, 1997

Our official team decal, 1997

Gennie and me at the Paris Finish Line, 1997

My gold medal, trophy and
Chinese driver's license

The BMW International Motorrad Rally, Tasmania 2000

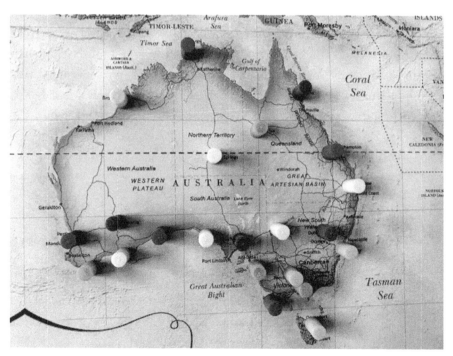

Some of the places I got to know, 1989-2008

CHAPTER 24

Taking Australia With Me

2001 – 2005

When I made the decision to recreate Australia in California, I knew that my future would not include Geoff Coat. The decision to officially end our relationship was made easier when I received a phone call from Geoff telling me that he had gone off his meds. "I don't need them anymore," he declared in a matter-of-fact way. I recognized this kind of behavior from my sister and how foolish it is when patients refuse to believe that it's their medication and/or counseling that's keeping them on an even keel. Rather than argue with Geoff, I decided to step back and acknowledge that Geoff would be responsible for himself. Many times in my life, I had assumed the role of caretaker as a way of trying to fix a problem that couldn't be fixed. Finally, I had learned that "No" is a complete sentence.

~~~

AS EAGER AS I WAS TO GET started on Glen Ellen, I'd had enough experience to know that this would be an extended project. It wouldn't be a matter of hiring an architect and setting him loose on the property. This would take months of contemplation, research, and artistic input. I called a contractor friend and asked him to look at the property. He suggested bringing in a trailer home, hooking up the utilities and adding a deck to make it livable so that I could spend a lot of time there absorbing the place. I thought that was a really good idea and I followed his advice.

Some of the work could be started right away like clearing away years of overgrown vegetation. My contractor friend took charge of that task as well and one afternoon I received an excited call from him. "Linda, we've just cleared a path to the water and you're not going to believe this creek." The very next day I was there viewing the gently flowing water of the Sonoma Creek which swirled and bubbled along the banks of the entire backside of the property. All I could say was "Amazing!" It reminded me of the wonderful summers I spent at my grandparents' Lake Mohawk cabin and I could envision children splashing in the clear waters of this enchanting creek. I instantly decided that the first permanent improvement I wanted to make was to build a stairway down to the creek at a spot which became known as "the beach."

Spending time in the trailer was a smart move. Sitting quietly on my deck I came to recognize the natural patterns of light and shadow and how the changing seasons affected the colors of the landscape. Slowly I began to visualize what I wanted. I knew for certain the architectural design would reflect an Australian aesthetic and the house would be the obvious repository of my substantial collection of paintings, sculptures, crafts, and furnishings. It was time to call in my wonderful Australian architect, Michael Rigg.

Michael Rigg was happy to come to Sonoma and spend some time, as I had, immersed in the beauty and ambience of the property. He felt the same passion I did about the evolution of Australian architecture and our collaboration was a perfect partnership. The style we agreed upon was best described as "Australian Homestead." Ultimately it would consist of six buildings — a new two-car garage with an attached work storage area, a main house, a guest house with a covered carport, a tower (art studio), a restored shed for motorcycles, and a hundred-year-old cabin down on the creek.

The main house was to be a wide rectangular structure with deep verandas wrapped around the entire exterior. In Australia, large water tanks set alongside houses for daily usage were a common feature. Early in my travels in Victoria, I remember being impressed by a modest square country home that had been built on top of four sizable rain tanks, one on each corner. I never forgot that clever idea, so my starting point for the main house was to have rain tanks under the front section of a complete wrap around veranda, six large tanks, three on each side of an impressive entry staircase. My initial decision to include them in the design was because of their aesthetics (especially when lit up at night) but I eventually realized their practical value. With fire danger in California an everyday threat, we decided to fit them to accommodate standard firehoses. This architectural decision would not only give the house a completely unique profile, it would also be exceedingly practical in that drought-risk environment.

As the plans for my homestead, were becoming more concrete, I realized I was going to have to find a local architect to carry out Michael's design because he wasn't licensed to work in California. I would need an architect who would be content to expedite the construction and be okay with not being on the creative team. I interviewed three local architects. The first one I contacted was based in San Francisco. He quickly dismissed me saying, "Get back to me when you are further along." The second, despite being told upfront that he would not be asked for creative input, promptly announced where he thought the main building should be placed. The third, Sean Montoya from Petaluma, knew all the county building rules and regulations, including who to call and who to pressure if things stalled. He promised, "I'll be your guy. I'll make sure it gets done. I'll prevent you from having to deal with the county roadblocks." I hired him on the spot.

WHEN IT CAME TIME TO consider the old Thompson house, my original impulse was to incorporate a portion of the existing house into the design. The more we examined the physical integrity of that aging structure, the clearer it became that the old house was beyond repair. In all my years of construction and remodeling I had never before dismantled a complete house. It was a troubling decision, but I had to make it. I instructed the demo crew to save the claw footed bathtub, four small decorative windows from the living room, the four redwood beams from the front porch and various outdoor light fixtures. I was determined to find a way to include them in the new house.

There's a certain magic that comes from linking the past to the present and when the buildings were completed, I had not only incorporated those original posts in the main house, I had placed the sweet bathtub in the guest house and affixed the outdoor lighting on the creek house. I made sure all wore brass plaques honoring their origins in the house built by George Thompson in the early 1900's.

To my delight in 2002, the project began moving forward more or less sequentially from building to building. The garage was the first structure built since it would provide a secure place for equipment and supplies while we completed the rest of the work. The exterior incorporated the kind of "quoins" stonework design that was found on many iconic South Australia buildings and instantaneously set the tone we were after.

In June 2002, construction of the "Tower" began. This was my attempt at being an architect. It was inspired by a two-story writer's cabin I had once seen in a Sunday *New York Times* article. The idea was to create a visual landmark on the edge of a serious ground drop toward the creek. It was a 14' x 35' tall steel construct with plexiglass and timber walls and a COR-TEN pyramidal roof. The top floor was designed with large sliding doors that opened onto a narrow balcony on the creek corner creating an observation area high in a tree, surrounded by nature. It didn't have running water and wasn't even airtight. It was a true "outbuilding," reminiscent of the old water towers on local California ranches. Because of its plexiglass panel reflections, during the day the Tower almost disappeared into the trees, sky, and foliage around it. At night, lit from the outside and within, the Tower looked like a beautiful glowing lantern. In time, it would become my art studio. A year or so after it was built, a visitor introduced me to the term "a Folly" which in the 2020 book, *Follies: An Architectural Journey*, author Rory

Fraser defines as "…an elaborate building set in a beautiful landscape that serves no purpose other than to improve the view: architecture for the sake of architecture." It would become much more but the term delighted me.

～

JANUARY 2003 MARKED the start of building number three, the guest house. Sonoma County guidelines for second living structures on a property limit the living space to a mere 960 square feet. Michael and I had already been challenged by similar dimensions with my Birdwood renovation in Australia and all of the furnishings from Birdwood would be exactly right for the guest house.

I imagined a scenario that consisted of a pioneer family homesteading on a piece of land, constructing their first home with a combination of local and relatively cheap materials. It would typically incorporate eucalyptus tree trunks, straw mixed with mud for walls, and manufactured light weight corrugated iron sheets which were easily transported across vast tracks of the outback and used for roofs and chimneys.

In the United States, early settlers who built log cabins chose to stack their tree trunks horizontally. In Australia, the method of stacking was vertical. I think it's safe to say I have one of the only vertically walled log cabins in the United States.

The first floor of the guest house, which consists of a living room and kitchen, features a vaulted roof which allows for a staircase that leads up to a cozy double bunk bedroom with a full bath. That design was stolen directly from my Lake Mohawk summers. Incorporated in the east facing roof are skylights which make mornings the highlight of the day.

Dividing the living area from the kitchen is a wheeled island which I had custom made for my Birdwood cottage. On one side are decorative and useful drawers and on the opposite side are barstools which face the TV in the living room. When entertaining, the island can be turned 180 degrees so that the stools are now on the living room side, allowing guests to face the kitchen, where the food preparer now has direct access to the storage drawers.

Just outside the kitchen-living area is the two-sided roofed veranda. The other two sides of the guest house have screened-in porches. One is off the mini-master bedroom, accessed through double French doors and features a large bathtub adapted from a farm animal trough. The second porch on the back of the cabin is what's known in Australia as a "sleep out." It serves a number of functions like bug-free dining and hanging out on a hammock during particularly warm days. The extra benefit is that these outdoor spaces provide additional square footage that is not counted as part of the County's allowable 960 square feet.

The final two years, June 2003 to September 2005, were devoted to completion of the main house. During that time, I lived in the guest house where I could stay closely involved in the building process, but even when I traveled, the work at Glen Ellen never stopped. I had been working with the same crew for four years and had complete confidence in them. The result is a magnificent three story, three bedroom, three and a half bath home that manages to be both grand and comfortably accommodating at the same time.

From the road, one would never guess the house contains three levels. Below the main floor a subterranean apartment lies hidden under the veranda. The top level with its vaulted roof line has an almost attic-like feel with roof dormers in the bedroom and a loft that overlooks the living room.

THE MOST JOYFUL PART of creating Glen Ellen was working with other artists. There's nothing as satisfying as discovering exactly the right person, the right piece, the right idea to fulfill your vision. Michael Rigg and I were always on the hunt for unique talents. We would talk about things we'd seen and liked and spend hours researching and poking about in shops to find some special inspiration. That's how we found Michael Retter and Tony Bishop, the two artists in Australia who created the amazing marquetry paneling in the billiards room.

In my early days in Australia, I visited Canberra, which is the Washington D. C. of Australia. I had little interest in going there, but as it turned out it was an amazing place to visit. The city itself was designed by the New York-based architectural firm of Mitchell/Giurgola. The first thing I noticed when I walked into the Parliament building was the scaled-up marquetry above our heads. It consisted of native floral motifs comprised of multi-sourced, inlaid wood in a variety of colors. It was a design element I wouldn't forget.

A billiard room is normally associated with dark paneling, but in my case I wanted it to be light in color and a bit more feminine. And that's when I suggested to Michael Rigg that we find someone to make some marquetry paneling similar to what I had seen in Canberra. Some weeks later, Michael Rigg walked into a souvenir shop in Western Australia and there were these small souvenirs of eucalyptus leaf marquetry. Michael asked the shopkeeper if this was the work of a local artist. She said, "No, he's up in Sydney, but here's his business card." It turned out it was Michael Retter. And when Michael Rigg called him, Michael Retter said, "Yes, I'm the man who makes the panels, but I need someone to design the motif." He recommended we get in touch with Tony Bishop the man he had worked with on the marquetry in the Canberra Parliament.

So, there they were, the two people whose work I so greatly admired, found by good old fashion luck. I personally met with Tony Bishop in Adelaide, not far from Birdwood, where we worked on the drawings together. The inspiration for our design was this lovely willow-like eucalyptus tree that was in my backyard on Canning Street. The panels were designed in Adelaide, handcrafted by 80-year-old Michael Retter in Sydney, and sent to Melbourne where they were crated and shipped to San Francisco.

When they arrived in Glen Ellen I was thrilled with the results. The miracle was that with all this moving around, there wasn't one ding or scratch on any of the panels. Watching them being installed was one of the most exciting days of the decorating process.

For the living room, I designed a rug based on a photograph I found in a coffee table book filled with aerial views of Australia. One day I was thumbing through it and saw this wonderful pre-desert area of Australia that is commonly known as The Bush. All these rich textures and shapes were naturally built into this aerial view which became my design. I knew of a store in South Yarra, Melbourne, which produced made-to-order carpets. I took that photo to the rug maker and said I wanted to duplicate this in about a 15' x 20' rug.

We were able to recreate some of the three-dimensionality of a landscape by using various materials, everything from wool to leather strips to silk with some subtle changes of forms and color in the patterns. It turned out to be absolutely perfect for the space. Viewed from the floor and the loft, there's hardly a time I or anyone else enters that room without noticing it.

Upon entering the front door, one cannot help but be gob smacked. Two staircases rise to the attic level and join in the middle. Hanging high above the landing where they meet is a slow turning ceiling fan. From the front door, you can look straight through the entry to the back set of French doors and see the backyard and a hint of the guest house. In a large cut out in the ceiling, a eucalyptus branch is suspended, complete with attached gum nuts collected from Michael Rigg's country property in Australia.

This unique feature was the result of two happy encounters. On a journey to the Outback, I came across a small arts and crafts shop where the owner had fashioned life-sized gum leaves from used corrugated iron. I had scooped up a handful to display in my Birdwood home. Early in the pre-planning phase of Glen Ellen, I was shown a local farmhouse and was struck by this family's solution for honoring a lovely birch tree which had been sacrificed in the construction of their house. They hung the tree so that it fit perfectly in the crook of a softly winding staircase and in the evening, it was lit with spotlights for dramatic effect.

That was the inspiration for my suspended eucalyptus/gum branch. I got back to the metal leaf maker and asked him to make me a bunch more leaves. My plan was to wire them to the branches and add low voltage string lamps. The leaf maker decided the project was too vast for him, so Michael and I put our heads together and found a window dresser from

Myer Department Store in Melbourne. She found just the right mini lights with shades the shape of gum nuts and used her faux painting skills to achieve the look I envisioned. Again, I held my breath during the uncrating and installation. Thankfully, not the tiniest twig was damaged. The final touches included nine Australian art works on the walls and Yarra timber on the floors. After all these years, I still enjoy being greeted by the sight and smell of Australia every time I open the front door.

AS THE HOUSE NEARED COMPLETION, I began dreaming about the housewarming party I would throw for all my friends and family. In my usual style, it would be memorable and would include a self-guided tour map for my nearly one hundred guests to discover the intricacies of the property on their own. The beauty of the plan was that I could enjoy being the hostess and not have to give individual tours to all the guests. To check out the viability of the plan, I decided to do a test-run by throwing a party for the people who had worked on the project. To my delight every one of them attended.

I was standing at the front door greeting my guests when this jaunty, 6'2" cowboy, in his eighties and dressed to the nines, came bounding up the front staircase and much to my surprise, picked me up and twirled me around. When he finally set me down, he said, "I'm your excavator. I'm the first man on the job, but I have never been invited to see a house that's finished."

The rest of the day, I overheard similar conversations between fathers and kids, even bookkeepers from various offices, saying they had never ever seen a finished project and they always were so curious as to how it finally turned out. They took pride in their work, but had all been left out of the pleasure of seeing the completion. After all they had given me, I was happy to give them back that simple gift. It was an exhausting day, but it was a very successful launch.

ONE MONTH LATER, I threw the big dedication party which was attended by ninety-five people. This time the event included all my friends and family. There were speeches by me and Michael Rigg and some of the other key people involved in the project and my Glen Ellen Homestead was launched and christened with all the pomp and circumstance worthy of such a unique and massive undertaking.

~~~

AT SOME POINT IN the process of recreating Australia in Sonoma, I couldn't deny that my entire life had been a series of putting one foot in front of the other, leading me to that moment and every other event shared in this memoir. The magnitude of the Glen Ellen project called on all my creative endeavors – art school, the development of my personal vision, the purchasing and renovation of a string of houses, learning about business – all of it came together in support of this project. Glen Ellen would not only be the repository of the extensive art and furnishings collection I had gathered in Australia, it would be a chronicle of my life, my creativity, and my experiences.

Just like the revelation I had years ago in my dank Bayview studio when I completed an unexpected work of art, I came to the realization that this was all going to happen… I was always going to make that mark, that gesture. I just didn't know it.

Over the years people have asked why I "gave up making art." What they considered art was painting and drawing. What they failed to see was that my artistic vision was three-dimensional and was expressed in the creation of spaces that encompassed people's lives. This was not a conscious choice. I never said, "This is the kind of woman artist I want to be." It was the road my life has taken; was always going to take… I just didn't know it.

My job was to trust.

~~~

IT'S BEEN MORE THAN twenty years since I first set eyes on my Glen Ellen retreat. It's become a visual testament to my love of adventure and my passion for the new-found homeland that became my summer-after-summer sojourn for over two decades. The patina of time has brought a beauty to the place beyond what I had imagined.

The house is now becoming recognized by students and educators as a unique architectural gem and plans are in the works for a history book, *What A Place For A Home* (with Arthur Dawson and Lorna Johnson), about me, and the original land owners, and also a documentary film, *Dear Australia*, about the creation of my Australian Homestead and the gratitude I have for the best place on earth. I don't know if anything written or filmed will capture what it took to make my dream a reality, but the beauty I encounter every time I walk through the front door assures me it was all worth it.

WHAT HAVE I LEARNED from this unique life? One thing for sure; there's nothing more powerful than conquering your fear. It gives you self-esteem and makes you realize that nothing can or should stop you. In all my decisions — to go to nursing school, to explore feminism, to study art, to ride a motorcycle, to travel the world, and to build my dream property — I faced my disappointments, fears and loves and survived them all. In doing so I learned to appreciate and be in awe of everything I encountered. As the mystic, Joseph Campbell wrote, "It's all marvelous!"

MY REWARD HAS BEEN a treasure of cherished memories. For most people that might be enough. What I've learned is that unknown forces direct me, keep me on the move, and won't ever let me rest on my laurels. Once again, as on the day I stood alone on the southern edge of the continent of Australia with all its beauty and majesty, I stand on a precipice facing the future, knowing I have the strength and the courage to take on whatever comes next.

Michael Rigg, RAIA, my Aussie architect and me at Glen Ellen, California, 2005.

My Australia in Sonoma, 2005

The Tower. My attempt at being an architect, 2005

ACKNOWLEDGMENTS

In a very particular order of importance, I want to thank my daughter, Maida. While I pined and whined over the years about succumbing to the many requests I've had to write a memoir and wrestled with my concerns about self-indulgence, it was a phone conversation with Maida in which she calmly said, "Mom, I think you should do it," that finally gave me the kick I needed to start writing.

My amazing, beautiful, athletic, and often funny daughter represents the best of her father, Larry Stupski, and me. Thank you, Larry, for your left-brain contributions (business, math, and athletic acumen). I gladly take credit for artistic creativity, design appreciation, and the love of renovating houses and turning them into welcoming homes.

My parents, Margo and H. Walter Dodwell, and my sister, Karen, who while seeing me more Martian than Earthly, tolerated me well enough and certainly provided chapters of their own in my life, although they might not have written them.

The top-notch Registered Nursing education I obtained at the Ann May School of Nursing in Neptune, New Jersey, prepared me at age twenty-one to take on greater responsibility in the medical world of cancer research, as a floor head nurse and as an IV Team creator. Similarly, in my late thirties, The San Francisco Art Institute provided five of my best years, in which I learned to be comfortable with and trusting of my inner voice.

Ann Toulmin-Rothe and Robert Baxter, the Westport, Connecticut, artists who provided me a bohemian haven and art classes and who pointed me in the direction of the San Francisco Art Institute.

Dennis Casey, a fellow student, confidant, and motorcycle mentor — the only man who appreciated and encouraged the risk taker in me. It was Dennis who suggested I book a flight to Australia, a move that significantly changed the course of my life.

Karen Armstrong, a BMW K bike rider, who took a chance on a very rookie rider, braved Spring Break in Baja Mexico, for getting me hooked on adventure and teaching me tricks and techniques that only a fellow woman biker would know.

Words will never suffice to explain my love and appreciation for all my Aussie mates.

Geoff Coat (Australian Motorcycle Touring Company), the sweetest man ever, who patiently taught me the art of motorcycling, who adored me as I had never been adored and cherished, and gracefully bowed out when the time came.

Pamela Bone, editor of *The Age* newspaper, who was the first person to encourage me to write my story. Kim and Ian Bear for insisting we be friends when I didn't know I needed them; Hugh and Joanne Irvine, fellow motorcyclists and pioneer IT experts, whose friendships were and are precious to me.

The motorcycle world provided numerous mentors and inspirations. Reading Ted Simon's book, *Jupiter's Travels*, assured me seeing the world on a motorcycle was doable and would never disappoint.

Two shout-outs to Burt Richmond (Lotus Motorcycle Tours of Chicago) and Werner and Carol Wachter (Edelweiss Bike Travel of Austria). Because of their early entries into the business of touring by motorcycle, I got to experience some of the forty countries I visited straddling a BMW R100 GS. Burt also must be credited for introducing me to Phillip Young's 2nd Annual 1997 Peking to Paris Vintage & Classic Motor Race. My co-driver Genevieve Obert, of Santa Cruz, CA. Her brilliant book, *Prince Borghese's Trail*, is a must if you want to get the whole story.

Architects Michael Rigg (Australia) and Shawn Montoya (California) who helped me create what I now refer to as the "Five acres, five years, five buildings, Glen Ellen, California enterprise." High fives to both of them for putting their egos aside for the good of the project. Ken Morita, the building contractor, for putting up with three "bosses" supervising upwards of a hundred workers, producing a true masterpiece and pleasing the lady boss beyond belief.

I want to thank each and every builder, project manager, contractor, artist, excavator, electrician, plumber, roofer, and clean-up crew on the U. S. East Coast/West Coast, and in Melbourne, VIC and Birdwood, SA, Australia. They and their talents were extraordinary. We don't celebrate them enough!

Special kudos to Ana Maria Pitta, my housekeeper and friend of twenty-five years, for all the time, devotion, and love she gave me, and to Marty Osborne, my property manager/historian, fellow brain stormer, and occasional shoulder-to-cry-on… you are The Best!

And a special thanks to Judy Chaikin and Loren Stephens, of the Write Wisdom team, for bringing me across the writing finish line. I truly could not and would not have done it without them! Thanks also to Tisha Morris for helping produce this memoir.

Made in the USA
Las Vegas, NV
25 February 2022

44502804R00132